SHORTCUT COOKING

The Earth-Friendly Energy-Saving Cookbook

Favorite Recipes® Press

BLANQUETTE OF CHICKEN

1 onion
6 whole cloves
1 stalk celery, chopped
1 carrot, chopped
1 bay leaf
1 chicken, cut up
$1/3$ cup flour
1 teaspoon salt
$1/8$ teaspoon pepper
$1/2$ teaspoon paprika
$1/2$ cup butter, melted
2 cups water
1 cup sliced celery
1 cup sliced carrot

1 9-ounce package frozen Italian beans, thawed
$1/3$ cup butter, melted
$1/3$ cup flour
1 teaspoon salt
$1/2$ teaspoon basil
$1/4$ teaspoon pepper
1 cup milk
1 $2^{1}/2$-ounce jar sliced mushrooms, drained
$1/4$ cup sliced pimento-stuffed green olives

Stud onion with cloves. Tie onion, 1 stalk celery, 1 carrot and bay leaf in cheesecloth to make bouquet garni. Coat chicken with mixture of $1/3$ cup flour, 1 teaspoon salt, $1/8$ teaspoon pepper and paprika. Brown in $1/2$ cup butter in skillet. Add water and bouquet garni. Simmer, covered, for 10 minutes. Add remaining vegetables. Simmer, covered, for 45 minutes or until chicken is tender. Combine $1/3$ cup butter, $1/3$ cup flour, 1 teaspoon salt, basil and $1/4$ teaspoon pepper in saucepan. Stir in milk. Cook until thickened, stirring constantly. Cook for 1 minute, stirring constantly. Arrange chicken and vegetables in serving dish. Reserve $1^{1}/2$ cups broth. Stir broth into thickened sauce. Bring to a boil, stirring constantly. Add mushrooms and olives. Pour over chicken. Yield: 6 servings.

(Photograph for this recipe is on the cover.)

Great American Opportunities, Inc./Favorite Recipes® Press

Essayist: Laura Hill
Cover Photograph: United Dairy Industry Association

This cookbook is a collection of our favorite recipes which are not necessarily original recipes.

Copyright© 1991 by: Great American Opportunities
P.O. Box 305142
Nashville, TN 37230

Library of Congress Catalog Number is: 91-16808
ISBN: 0-87197-302-2
Manufactured in the United States of America
First Printing: 1991, 33,000 copies   Second Printing: 1991, 39,000 copies
Third Printing: 1992, 32,000 copies   Fourth Printing: 1992, 21,000 copies
Fifth Printing: 1992, 42,000 copies

Contents

The Earth-Friendly Kitchen

One of the great problems of American life in the last few years of the 20th century is that, while development and progress have brought us nearly unheard of affluence, they have also posed a terrible threat to our basic treasure, the Earth.

In a short period of time, terms like global warming, greenhouse effect and tropical deforestation have become commonplace in our language. Even school children understand the ecological crisis on a surprisingly sophisticated level. Recycling has now become a favorite weekend sport for American families.

Perhaps the approach of a new century has helped prompt the rapid growth of this green revolution. Or perhaps it is, hopefully not too late, the realization that Mother Earth is not necessarily immortal—certainly not without the loving care of us all.

In the United States, no group of people is more interested in protecting the fragile balance of the earth's ecology than those of us who buy and prepare most of the food that America eats. After all, feeding people is the most basic kind of nurturing—and isn't that what environmental protection really is all about?

Anyone who's spent much time in the supermarket has questioned the processes that bring us tomatoes way out of season. We've wondered at the mountains of plastic and aluminum that result from even a quick trip to the store. And we've seen such delicacies as fresh salmon disappear from the store after a major oil spill and piles of Alar-sprayed apples go uneaten.

Daily we become more educated about—and more alarmed by—what decades of neglect and abuse have done to the Earth. Most of us have made at least some effort to do our part.

At the same time, the realities of life leave us little enough time to plan meals, shop, prepare food and eat. We have little time for recycling or reading about the ins and outs of organic gardening. We want to help, but for many of us, time is a real problem.

In this book, *Shortcut Cooking*, we've brought together

your concerns about lifestyle and the environment. We include recipes and menu ideas that are simple to prepare in a small amount of time, yet are earth-friendly choices. You can avoid prepackaged goods, greasy styrofoamed fast food and unhealthy and environmentally costly meals. We think you'll find these are an agreeable way to live conveniently while you do something nice for the planet.

What, Me Pollute?

Your kitchen may seem far away from the disappearing rain forests in Brazil, but we've come to realize the complicated links between all of us and the way we live. In fact, **the average American kitchen is the location of an alarming amount of the damage to our environment**.

THE CHEF

Take a look at that mountain of plastic and tin cans again. **The United States generates twice as much solid waste per capita as any other country in the world.** It recycles little—about 20 percent of its total (compared to 50 percent in Japan). One estimate of our garbage output notes that in 1987 this country produced enough garbage to fill a one-foot deep, 24-lane highway from Boston to Los Angeles. The vast majority of all this waste goes into landfills. Thousands of them have closed or are closing in the next 10 years. As the garbage sits in landfills, it slowly leaks contaminants into the earth, polluting ground water. But if it is burned, it releases pollution into our air. Dumped in the ocean, plastic garbage washes up onto our beaches, or destroys ocean wildlife.

The Earth's air is full of contaminants caused by our increasing use of fossil fuels. The damage to the ozone layer is caused by chemical pollutants. This creates a frightening trend toward global warming. Some scientists predict a major crisis for the earth's future.

Our diet also helps create an ecological crisis. It has been estimated that we Americans eat nearly twice as much protein as we need every day. This protein- and fat- heavy diet is responsible for a host of health problems. It takes a heavy toll on the earth. To raise one pound of beef, some 16 pounds of plant matter must be used. This requires that more and more land be set aside for livestock grazing.

The Homemade Pollution Solution

If the news is this bad, what can one modest cook do to help? The answer is: *plenty*!

We're not suggesting that you give your life over to composting and trash sorting. But on a day-to-day basis, even the "shortcut cook" can do his or her bit for the planet. And most of it takes no time at all, but produces large benefits.

The logical place to begin is in your kitchen—the environmental crisis center of our homes. Take a look around and you'll see why.

- The major energy-using appliances are in your kitchen.
- Most of your garbage is produced right here.
- A large portion of the water your family uses is used here.
- Toxic chemicals are stored in the kitchen.
- Your diet is determined and prepared here.

Appliances are a primary concern in environmentally-conscious households. It would be nice to be able to start over with energy-efficient refrigerators, stoves and dishwashers. If you do buy new appliances, you may be surprised to learn that self-cleaning ovens use little electricity because they are so well insulated. And they are cheaper and less toxic to clean electrically than with commercial oven cleaner. On gas stoves, choose electronic ignitions, which use less fuel than pilot lights.

But even if you're going to keep your old appliances for a while, you can save energy. When you cook, keep the flame just touching the bottom of the pan or lower (a higher flame wastes gas). On **electric stoves**, use burners which are the same size or smaller than the pot you're using. Turn off the heat just before you're done to let residual heat finish your cooking. Use lids on your pots.

Arrange **oven racks** before turning on the oven—it saves heat. Do not preheat unless you're baking; it's not necessary for roasts or casseroles and it wastes energy. And no peaking. Each time the oven door opens, 25 degrees of heat is lost.

For small quantities of food, a **microwave** is most efficient. Larger quantities, though, are better prepared in a conventional oven. Consider using a pressure cooker, which takes up to two-thirds less time to cook, saving energy.

The key to keeping a **refrigerator** earth-friendly is to keep it in top working condition. Keep gaskets in good repair. For efficiency's sake, keep a refrigerator set to 34 to 40 degrees, the freezer at about 0 degrees. Keep coils clean and defrost the freezer frequently; they will have to work less to keep cooler. A refrigerator works most efficiently when it is fuller, but leave ample room around items so the cool air can easily circulate.

Good news! It's more energy efficient to use a **dishwasher** than to wash dishes by hand. A dishwasher uses less hot water. Always wait to use the dishwasher until it's full (it takes the same amount of energy and water to wash one dish as to wash a whole load). Whenever possible, let dishes air dry. Try using less detergent. Unless you have very hard water, you do not need to always fill the detergent cup.

It's in the Bag

Now let's talk about shopping. There are some basic earth-friendly principles to keep in mind when you hit the supermarket. Your mother practiced many of these during the good old preconvenience-food days. **Buy less**—the less you consume, the less you ask of the environment. **Eat lower**

on the food chain, stressing more grains and veggies, which are easier on the environment (not to mention your arteries and waistline). **Buy smart**—no ozone-destroying aerosols, non-degradable styrofoam products, or extra paper goods (especially those that are chlorine bleached). **Buy in-season** foods that are locally grown (they didn't cost as much energy to produce and transport). Ask for produce grown without pesticides.

Avoid excess packaging. About 10 percent of your grocery bill goes for packaging. It does little more than become part of the 4 pounds of garbage per person per day we produce. **Look for cardboard packaging** (much of which is made from recycled paper). When you can, buy in big lots for more product and less package. **Bring your own bags** with you —cloth, brown paper or simply the plastic bags you took home the times before.

Hold the Mayo (Jar)

O nce you get all this home, keep in mind the two big R's: **Reuse** and **Recycle**. These are lessons most of our parents and grandparents learned during the Depression. We are realizing the value of these lessons once again.

Want a see-through, washable, sealable container that you can use in the microwave? One that lasts for years? Is free? One that is biodegradable? **Try reusing your mayonnaise, pickle and jelly jars**. Use egg cartons (you did buy the cardboard type, didn't you?) to store flower bulbs and other small items. You remember—there really was life before Tupperware®.

Do try recycling at home. It could be just separating

newspapers or cans from the rest of the trash and taking them to your neighborhood recycling center. It may take a little family retraining. For example, one husband sneaked bags of recyclables out to the curb with the rest of the garbage only to receive a stern lecture from his nine-year-old daughter the next day. There are dozens of clever home "recycling centers" to choose from in stores and catalogs. **Set aside the place** and discuss with your family the reasons why we must recycle. Get some helpful information from your community recycling group or office. Just start! In a surprisingly short time, recycling becomes part of the household routine. Every member of the family, even little tots, will quickly come to understand.

It's Your Serve

Ordering fast food is no more time-saving, really, than using up what's in the refrigerator. For emergencies, keep a prepacked bag lunch in the freezer and skip the store-bought burger. Save the heels of bread and those longer single hotdog buns and store them in a bag in the freezer for fresh bread crumbs.

In every 10 pounds of garbage we throw away, experts estimate, there are several pounds of recyclable food. Why not resurrect the old-fashioned left-over buffet supper on Sunday night? It's a great way to save money and cooking time while you clean out the refrigerator for the next week. And when you **don't waste food**, you **don't waste the energy**, the land that grew it, or the resources it takes to dispose of it.

If you don't **grow your own food** already, try it. A little patio garden or a small herb bed will bring you pleasure and help the atmosphere. **Avoid pesticides** that pollute in favor of non-toxic, organic products. Help **maintain a bird population** in your yard for natural insect control. **Water thoughtfully**, and **mulch** to retain moisture. **Learn to compost**—it's easier than you think.

Are you ready to change your habits? Are you ready to become earth-friendly? With most new things, the key is to **start small**, doing what you can as you can. Remember that at one time in your life brushing your teeth and tying your shoes were new challenges. Now they are habits. **Love your Earth and save it for your children.** You'll thank yourself and so will your children.

Nutritional Analysis Guidelines

The editors have attempted to present these family recipes in a form that allows approximate nutritional values to be computed. Persons with dietary or health problems or whose diets require close monitoring should not rely solely on the nutritional information provided. They should consult their physicians or a registered dietitian for specific information.

Abbreviations for Nutritional Analysis

Cal — Calories	Fiber — Dietary Fiber	Sod — Sodium
Prot — Protein	T Fat — Total Fat	gr — gram
Carbo — Carbohydrates	Chol — Cholesterol	mg — milligrams

Nutritional information for these recipes is computed from information derived from many sources, including materials supplied by the United States Department of Agriculture, computer databanks and journals in which the information is assumed to be in the public domain. However, many specialty items, new products and processed foods may not be available from these sources or may vary from the average values used in these analyses. More information on new and/or specific products may be obtained by reading the nutrient labels. Unless otherwise specified, the nutritional analysis of these recipes is based on level measurements and the following standards.

- **Artificial sweeteners** vary in use and strength so should be used "to taste," using the recipe ingredients as a guideline.
- **Artificial sweeteners** using aspertame (NutraSweet and Equal) should not be used as a sweetener in recipes involving prolonged heating which reduces the sweet taste. For further information on the use of these sweeteners, refer to package information.
- **Alcoholic ingredients** have been analyzed for the basic ingredients, although cooking causes the evaporation of alcohol thus decreasing the caloric content.
- **Buttermilk**, **sour cream** and **yogurt** are the types available commercially.
- **Cake mixes** prepared using package directions include 3 eggs and 1/2 cup oil.
- **Chicken**, cooked for boning and chopping, has been roasted; this method yields the lowest caloric values.
- **Cottage cheese** is cream-style with 4.2% creaming mixture. Dry-curd cottage cheese has no creaming mixture.
- **Eggs** are all large.
- **Flour** is unsifted all-purpose flour.
- **Garnishes**, serving suggestions and other optional additions and variations are not included in the analysis.
- **Margarine** and **butter** are regular, not whipped or presoftened.
- **Milk** is whole milk, 3.5% butterfat. Lowfat milk is 1% butterfat. Evaporated milk is whole milk with 60% of the water removed.
- **Oil** is any type of vegetable oil. Shortening is hydrogenated vegetable shortening.
- **Salt** and other ingredients to taste have not been included in the analysis.
- If an ingredient shows a variable amount, the analysis reflects the larger.

Shortcuts To Meal Making

The Well-Stocked Pantry

O ne of the secrets of saving time in food preparation is cutting down on trips to the market. That, however, requires planning. It requires knowing what items are in your pantry and making a shopping list for restocking your pantry. That may require backing up still one more step to the question "What should a well-stocked pantry include?" Remember that the "pantry" includes not only the shelves in the cabinets and closet but also the refrigerator and freezer or anywhere that food items can be stored. This is a list of suggestions for the well-stocked pantry:

Dry Products	
flour	spaghetti
sugar	rice
brown sugar	soup mixes
confectioners' sugar	cake mixes
baking mix	crackers
cornmeal	pudding mixes
corn muffin and other mixes	dry milk powder
graham cracker pie shells	dry buttermilk powder
dry bread crumbs	coffee
salt	tea
pepper	taco shells
cloves	Parmesan cheese
nutmeg	seasoning and salad
ginger	dressing mixes
basil	gelatins, flavored and
oregano	unflavored
garlic and onion powder	popcorn
garlic and onion salt	cereals
Italian seasoning	baking powder
macaroni	bouillon cubes
noodles	baking cocoa

Canned and Bottled Products

assorted vegetables	vinegar
assorted fruits	molasses
tuna	honey
ham	mayonnaise/mustard
chicken	catsup
cream soups	horseradish
cheese soup	barbecue sauce
chicken broth	taco sauce
evaporated milk	salad dressings
sweetened condensed milk	jam and jelly
tomato sauce	maple syrup
soy sauce	canned frosting
Worcestershire sauce	spaghetti sauce
steak sauce	pie filling
cooking oil	pickles and olives
olive oil	peanut butter
chili sauce	vanilla extract

Frozen Products

assorted vegetables	waffles/pancakes
assorted fruits	assorted meat, poultry
juice concentrates	and seafood
pie shells	ice cream
whipped topping	bread dough

Refrigerated Products

eggs	sour cream
milk	assorted cheeses
margarine/butter	salad vegetables
cream cheese	bacon/ham/sausage

A Month of Main Dishes

For maximum efficiency, you should purchase as much food as you can at one time. The time and money saved in planning meals and shopping for them is well worth the initial time and expense. The following shopping list will provide everything you will need for the month of main dishes in our chapter beginning on page 45. Just add a vegetable, salad and bread. Plan to freeze ground beef in one-pound packets; freeze seafood and deli foods; chop and freeze green peppers, etc. Use perishables like zucchini the first week.

Shopping List

Meats
Beef
   2 pounds round steak
   4 minute steaks
   1 3-pound sirloin tip roast
   1 pound boneless sirloin
   7 pounds ground beef
Ham
   6 4-ounce ham steaks
   1 5-pound canned ham
Pork
   14 pork chops
   ½ pound bacon
   2 pounds kielbasa sausage

Poultry
Chicken
   4 chicken breasts
   10 chicken breast filets
   3 pounds chicken pieces
   4 chicken breast quarters
   1 5-ounce can chicken
Turkey
   2 pounds deli turkey

Seafood
   1 16-ounce can clams

1 pound frozen fish filets
1 10-ounce package frozen
   cooked shrimp
1 pound orange roughy filets

Soups
   3 packages (6 envelopes) dry
      onion soup mix
   4 cans cream of mushroom
      soup
   1 can cream of potato soup
   1 can Cheddar cheese soup
   2 cans cream of chicken soup
   1 can cream of celery soup
   Chicken and beef bouillon
      cubes

Vegetables
Canned
   4 4-ounce cans mushrooms
   1 14-ounce can potatoes
   3 8-ounce cans tomato
      sauce
   2 3-ounce cans French-
      fried onions
   2 20-ounce cans tomatoes
      (1 Italian)

Shopping List (continued)

Frozen
  2 10-ounce packages
     broccoli
  1 10-ounce package Bird's
     Eye Chinese vegetables
  1 16-ounce package mixed
     broccoli, corn and red
     pepper
  1 24-ounce package
     hashed brown potatoes
  1 10-ounce package
     frozen peas
Fresh
  8 carrots
  10 potatoes
  5 green bell peppers
  1 red bell pepper
  2 bunches broccoli
  6 onions
  1 bunch celery
  6 zucchini
Other
  1 16-ounce package rice
  1 small package minute rice
  1 20-ounce can pineapple
     chunks
  1 20-ounce can sliced
     pineapple

Bread Products
  1 6-ounce package corn
     muffin mix
  1 16-ounce loaf French bread
  1 16-ounce loaf white bread
  1 pie shell
  1 12-ounce package Ritz
     crackers
  1 small package baking
     mix
  2 packages stuffing mix
  1 package corn bread stuffing
     mix
  1 2-pound package spaghetti
  1 16-ounce package linguine

  1 8-count can crescent rolls
  1 small can dry bread crumbs

Dairy Products
  2 12-ounce cans evaporated
     milk
  2¹/₂ pounds Cheddar cheese
  3 cups sour cream
  12 ounces American cheese
  1 4-ounce can Parmesan
     cheese
  4 ounces blue cheese

Miscellaneous
  1 envelope brown gravy mix
  1 envelope chili seasoning mix
  16 ounces ginger ale
  1 10-ounce jar currant jelly
  1 8-ounce bottle of Italian
     salad dressing
  1 2-ounce jar pimento
  1 2-ounce jar olives

Pantry Items
  eggs
  milk
  margarine
  flour
  sugar and brown sugar
  salt and pepper
  oil and olive oil
  chili sauce
  baking powder
  vinegar
  molasses and honey
  steak sauce
  mayonnaise and mustard
  soy sauce
  cornstarch
  garlic
  Worcestershire sauce
  horseradish
  lemon juice
  spices

Make-Ahead Mixes

All of us have discovered the time-saving magic of prepared mixes and convenience foods. The best mixes, however, are the ones you prepare yourself. They take a little time to prepare, but they save time, money, energy and packaging in the long run and are so easy and convenient for that busy-day dinner.

HERBED SEASONING MIX

2 cups Parmesan cheese
1/2 cup sesame seed
2 tablespoons poppy
  seed
3 tablespoons celery seed
1 tablespoon onion flakes

2 tablespoons parsley
  flakes
1/2 teaspoon dillseed
1/2 teaspoon garlic salt
2 teaspoons paprika
1/2 teaspoon pepper

Combine all ingredients in bowl; mix well. Store in airtight container. Sprinkle over salads or baked potatoes. Yield: 3 cups.

Herbed Sour Cream Dip—Combine 2 tablespoons mix with 1 cup sour cream in bowl; mix well. Chill for 1 hour. Serve with fresh vegetables or crackers. Yield: 1 cup.

RANCH SALAD DRESSING MIX

8 teaspoons onion flakes   1/4 cup parsley flakes
1/2 teaspoon garlic powder

Combine onion flakes, garlic powder and parsley flakes in bowl; mix well. Store in airtight container. Yield: 1/4 cup.

Ranch Salad Dressing—Combine 2 tablespoons mix with 1 cup mayonnaise and 1 cup buttermilk or sour cream for dressing or dip. Yield: 2 cups.

FRENCH SALAD DRESSING MIX

2/3 cup sugar
2 teaspoons onion flakes

2 teaspoons dry mustard
2 teaspoons paprika

Combine sugar, onion flakes, dry mustard and paprika in bowl; mix well. Store in airtight container. Yield: 1 cup.

French Salad Dressing—Mix 1/2 cup mix, 3/4 cup oil and 1/4 cup vinegar in jar. Chill for 1 hour. Yield: 1 1/4 cups.

SPICY RICE MIX

5 cups uncooked rice
5 teaspoons instant
   chicken bouillon

5 envelopes onion soup
   mix

Combine rice, bouillon and soup mix in bowl; mix well. Store in airtight container. Yield: 6 cups.

Spicy Rice Casserole—Sauté 1 1/2 cups mix in 3/4 cup margarine in skillet until brown. Combine with 2 1/4 cups hot water in 2-quart baking dish. Bake, covered, at 350 degrees for 1 hour. Yield: 4 servings.

BASIC PANCAKE MIX

10 cups flour
2 1/2 cups nonfat dry milk
1/2 cup sugar

1/4 cup baking powder
1 tablespoon salt

Combine flour, dry milk, sugar, baking powder and salt in bowl; mix well. Store in airtight container. Yield: 13 cups.

Easy Pancakes—Combine 1 1/2 cups mix, 1 egg, 3 tablespoons oil and 1 cup water in bowl; mix well. Bake on hot greased griddle. Yield: 12 pancakes.

Puffy Pancake—Combine 2/3 cup mix, 4 eggs and 2/3 cup milk in blender container; process until smooth. Pour into 1/4 cup melted margarine in pie plate. Bake at 450 degrees for 18 minutes. Yield: 6 servings.

WHOLE GRAIN PANCAKE MIX

8 cups whole wheat flour
2 cups nonfat dry milk
3 tablespoons baking
powder

3 cups oats
2 teaspoons sugar
1 tablespoon salt

Combine flour, dry milk, baking powder, oats, sugar and salt in bowl; mix well. Store in airtight container. Yield: 12 cups.

Healthy Pancakes—Combine 1 1/2 cups mix with 1 egg, 1 1/4 cups milk, 1 tablespoon oil and 1 tablespoon honey in bowl; mix well. Bake on hot greased griddle. Yield: 12 pancakes.

CORNMEAL MIX

4 1/2 cups cornmeal
4 cups sifted flour
1/2 cup sugar (optional)

1/3 cup baking powder
2 teaspoons salt
1 cup shortening

Combine cornmeal, flour, sugar, baking powder and salt in large bowl; mix well. Cut in shortening until crumbly. Store in covered container at room temperature. Yield: 12 cups.

Easy Corn Bread—Combine 2 1/2 cups mix with 1 egg and 1 cup milk in bowl; beat for 1 minute. Pour into greased 8x8-inch baking pan. Bake at 425 degrees for 20 to 25 minutes or until golden brown. Yield: 8 servings.

Corn Muffins—Combine 3 cups mix with 1 beaten egg and 1 1/4 cups milk in bowl; mix just until moistened. Fill greased muffin cups 2/3 full. Bake at 425 degrees for 12 to 15 minutes or until golden brown. Yield: 12 muffins.

Cornmeal Griddle Cakes—Combine 3 cups mix with 2 eggs and 1 3/4 cups milk in bowl; mix well. Bake on hot lightly greased griddle. Yield: 12 griddle cakes.

BASIC CAKE MIX

8 cups cake flour
6 cups sugar
1/4 cup baking powder

1 teaspoon salt
2 1/2 cups shortening

Sift flour, sugar, baking powder and salt into bowl. Cut in shortening until crumbly. Store in airtight container. Yield: 15 cups.

Buttermilk Chocolate Cake—Combine 3 1/2 cups basic mix, 1/2 cup sugar, 2 eggs and 1 cup buttermilk in bowl; mix well. Mix 1/2 cup baking cocoa, 1 teaspoon soda, 1 teaspoon vanilla and 1/2 cup boiling water in small bowl. Add to batter; mix well. Spoon into 2 greased and floured 8-inch round cake pans. Bake at 350 degrees for 10 minutes. Increase temperature to 375 degrees. Bake for 20 minutes. Cool in pans for 20 minutes. Remove to wire rack to cool completely. Frost with favorite chocolate frosting. Yield: 8 servings.

Spice Cake—Mix 3 1/3 cups basic mix, 1 teaspoon nutmeg, 1 teaspoon cinnamon and 1/2 teaspoon cloves in large bowl. Bring 1/4 cup butter, 1 cup packed brown sugar and 1 cup water to a boil in saucepan. Add to dry ingredients; mix well. Add 1/2 cup sour cream, 2 eggs and 1/2 cup chopped nuts; mix well. Spoon into greased and floured 10x15-inch cake pan. Bake at 375 degrees for 20 to 25 minutes or until cake tests done. Cool completely. Frost with favorite caramel nut frosting. Yield: 16 servings.

Southern Pound Cake—Combine 3 1/2 cups basic mix, one 4-ounce package vanilla instant pudding mix, 1/2 cup oil, 1 cup milk and 1 teaspoon vanilla in mixer bowl. Beat at medium speed for 4 minutes. Beat in 4 eggs 1 at a time. Spoon into greased and floured bundt pan. Bake at 350 degrees for 45 to 55 minutes or until cake tests done. Cool in pan for 10 minutes. Remove to wire rack to cool completely. Dust with confectioners' sugar. Yield: 16 servings.

MASTER BAKING MIX

9 cups sifted flour
1/3 cup baking powder
1/4 cup sugar
1 tablespoon salt

2 teaspoons cream of
tartar
2 cups shortening

Sift flour, baking powder, sugar, salt and cream of tartar together 3 times. Cut in shortening until crumbly. Store in airtight container at room temperature. Yield: 13 cups.

Quick Biscuits—Combine 2 cups mix and 2/3 cup milk in bowl; mix lightly. Knead 10 times on floured surface. Pat 1/2 inch thick; cut with biscuit cutter. Place on baking sheet. Bake at 425 degrees for 10 to 12 minutes.
Yield: 10 biscuits.

Buttered Breadsticks—Combine 2 cups mix with 1/2 cup milk in bowl; mix well. Knead 10 times on floured surface. Roll into rectangle; cut into 32 strips. Brush with melted butter; place in baking pan. Bake at 400 degrees for 12 minutes or until golden brown. Yield: 32 breadsticks.

Cheese Pinwheels—Combine 3 cups mix with 1 cup water in bowl; mix well. Roll thin on floured surface. Sprinkle with 3/4 cup shredded Cheddar cheese. Roll as for jelly toll. Cut into 1/4-inch slices; place on baking sheet. Bake at 350 degrees for 10 minutes. Yield: 40 pinwheels.

Fluffy Dumplings—Combine 2 cups mix and 1/2 cup milk in bowl; mix just until moistened. Drop by tablespoonfuls into hot stew, soup or fruit sauce. Steam for 12 minutes.

Golden Waffles—Combine 2 cups mix and 2 tablespoons sugar in bowl. Add mixture of 1 cup milk, 1/4 cup oil and 2 egg yolks; mix until moistened. Fold in 2 stiffly beaten egg whites. Bake in hot waffle iron. Yield: 6 waffles.

Quick Muffins—Combine 3 cups mix and 2 tablespoons sugar in bowl. Add mixture of 1 cup milk and 1 egg; mix until moistened. Spoon into greased muffin cups. Bake at 425 degrees for 20 minutes or until golden brown.
Yield: 10 muffins.

Easy Coffee Cakes—Combine 3 cups mix and 1/2 cup sugar in bowl. Add mixture of 2/3 cup milk and 1 egg; mix until moistened. Pour into 2 greased 9-inch pans. Bake at 350 degrees for 30 minutes or until golden brown. Yield: 12 servings.

Apple Nut Cake—Combine 2 1/3 cups mix, 1 cup packed brown sugar, 1 teaspoon cinnamon and 1 teaspoon cloves in bowl; mix well. Beat in 2 eggs and 1/4 cup milk. Stir in 2 cups chopped apples and 1/2 cup chopped nuts. Bake in greased 8-inch pan at 375 degrees for 40 minutes or until cake tests done. Yield: 8 servings.

BRAN MUFFIN MIX

2 cups All-Bran cereal
2 cups boiling water
2 cups sugar
1 cup shortening
1 quart buttermilk

4 eggs, beaten
4 cups Bran Buds cereal
5 cups sifted flour
5 teaspoons soda

Combine All-Bran with boiling water in large bowl; let stand until cool. Cream sugar and shortening in mixer bowl until light. Add buttermilk, eggs and cereals; mix well. Sift in flour and soda; mix well. Store, covered, in refrigerator for up to 6 weeks.
Yield: 15 cups or enough for 5 dozen muffins.

Basic Muffins—Fill greased muffin cups 2/3 full. Bake at 350 degrees for 20 minutes.

Apple Bran Muffins—Combine 2 cups mix with 1/2 cup chopped apple and 1/2 teaspoon cinnamon. Bake as above.

Banana Bran Muffins—Combine 2 cups mix with 1 cup mashed banana. Bake as above.

Date and Nut Bran Muffins—Combine 2 cups mix with 1/4 cup each chopped dates and nuts. Bake as above.

Raisin Bran Muffins—Combine 2 cups mix with 1/4 cup raisins. Bake as above.

BASIC COOKIE MIX

8 cups flour	2 teaspoons salt
2¹/₂ cups sugar	1¹/₂ teaspoons soda
2 cups packed brown sugar	3 cups shortening

Combine flour, sugar, brown sugar, salt and soda in bowl; mix well. Cut in shortening until crumbly. Store in airtight container. Yield: 16 cups.

Chocolate Chip Cookies—Combine 3 cups cookie mix with 3 tablespoons milk, 1 teaspoon vanilla, 1 egg, 1 cup chocolate chips and ¹/₂ cup chopped pecans in bowl; mix well. Drop by teaspoonfuls onto greased cookie sheet. Bake at 375 degrees for 10 to 15 minutes or until golden brown. Yield: 3 dozen.

Peanut Butter Cookies—Combine 3 cups cookie mix, ¹/₄ cup packed brown sugar, 2 eggs, ¹/₂ cup chunky peanut butter and 1 teaspoon vanilla in bowl; mix well. Shape into 1-inch balls; place on greased cookie sheet. Press with fork to flatten. Bake at 375 degrees for 10 to 12 minutes or until light brown. Yield: 3 dozen.

Spice Cookies—Combine 2 cups cookie mix with ¹/₄ cup molasses, ¹/₂ teaspoon vanilla and ¹/₂ teaspoon each ginger, cinnamon and allspice in bowl; mix well. Drop by teaspoonfuls onto greased cookie sheet. Flatten with buttered glass dipped in sugar. Bake at 375 degrees for 8 to 10 minutes or until edges are brown. Yield: 2 dozen.

Snickerdoodles—Combine 2¹/₂ cups cookie mix with ¹/₄ teaspoon soda, 1 teaspoon cream of tartar and 1 egg in bowl; mix well. Shape into 1¹/₂-inch balls. Roll in cinnamon-sugar, coating well. Place on cookie sheet. Bake at 400 degrees for 8 to 10 minutes or until light brown. Yield: 2¹/₄ dozen.

BASIC ITALIAN SAUCE

5 cups chopped onions
5 cups chopped green
  bell peppers
10 15-ounce cans
  tomato sauce
10 12-ounce cans
  tomato paste
1/4 cup sugar

10 envelopes spaghetti
  sauce mix
1 16-ounce can ripe
  olives, chopped
2 teaspoons oregano
3 bay leaves
15 cups water

Combine onions, green peppers, tomato sauce, tomato paste, sugar, spaghetti sauce mix, olives, oregano, bay leaves and water in stockpot; mix well. Simmer for 1 1/2 to 2 hours, stirring occasionally. Remove bay leaves. Store in meal-sized portions in freezer. Yield: 18 pints.

Basic Meat Sauce—Add browned ground beef to basic Italian sauce as desired.

Pizza Casserole—Alternate layers of 2 cups cooked macaroni, 1 1/2 cups shredded Cheddar cheese and 2 cups basic sauce in baking dish. Bake at 400 degrees for 30 minutes. Top with 1 cup shredded mozzarella cheese. Bake for 15 minutes longer. Yield: 4 servings.

Spaghetti Pie—Combine 3 cups hot cooked spaghetti, 2 tablespoons butter and 1/2 cup Parmesan in cheese in buttered pie plate; shape as for pie shell. Layer 1 cup cottage cheese and 1 1/2 cups basic meat sauce into spaghetti shell. Bake at 350 degrees for 20 minutes. Top with 1/2 cup shredded mozzarella cheese. Bake for 5 minutes. Yield: 4 servings.

Veal Parmigiana—Brown 4 veal patties in a small amount of oil in heavy skillet. Spoon 1 cup basic sauce and half of 1 drained 8-ounce can mushrooms into 8x12-inch baking dish. Arrange veal patties over top; sprinkle with oregano. Top with provolone cheese. Pour additional 1 cup basic sauce over top. Sprinkle with remaining mushrooms and Parmesan cheese. Bake at 350 degrees for 35 to 40 minutes or until bubbly. Yield: 4 servings.

HOT CHOCOLATE MIX

1 25-ounce package
nonfat dry milk
1 6-ounce jar nondairy
creamer

2 cups confectioners'
sugar
1 16-ounce can instant
chocolate drink mix

Combine dry milk, creamer, confectioners' sugar and drink mix in large bowl; mix well. Store in airtight container. Yield: 17 cups.

Hot Chocolate—Combine 3 tablespoons mix with 1 cup boiling water in cup; mix well. Yield: 1 serving.

SPICED COFFEE MIX

1/2 cup freeze-dried coffee
1/2 cup sugar

1/2 teaspoon nutmeg
1/2 teaspoon cinnamon

Combine coffee, sugar and spices in blender container; process for 30 seconds. Store in airtight container. Yield: 1 cup.

Spiced Coffee—Combine 1 to 2 teaspoons mix with 2/3 cup boiling water in cup; mix well. Yield: 1 serving.

RUSSIAN ZINGER MIX

2 cups orange drink mix
1 3-ounce package
sweetened lemonade
mix

1 1/3 cups sugar
1 teaspoon cinnamon
1/2 teaspoon cloves

Combine orange drink mix, lemonade mix, sugar and spices in bowl; mix well. Store in airtight container. Yield: 3 1/2 cups.

Russian Zinger—Combine 2 to 3 teaspoons mix with 1 cup boiling water in cup; mix well. Yield: 1 serving.

Quick
Appetizers

RANCH CHEESE BALL

1 cup shredded Cheddar
cheese
6 ounces cream cheese
1 envelope ranch salad
dressing mix

$1/2$ cup mayonnaise
$1/2$ cup milk
5 ounces sliced almonds,
toasted

Let Cheddar cheese and cream cheese stand at room temperature for 1 hour. Combine salad dressing mix, mayonnaise and milk in mixer bowl; mix well. Add cream cheese; beat until smooth. Add Cheddar cheese; mix well. Chill, covered, in freezer for 30 minutes. Shape into ball; coat with almonds. Yield: 16 servings.

Approx Per Serving: Cal 176; Prot 5 g; Carbo 4 g; Fiber 1 g;
T Fat 16 g; Chol 24 mg; Sod 240 mg.

HOT CHEESE CANAPÉS

$1^1/2$ cups shredded sharp
Cheddar cheese
1 cup mayonnaise
$1/2$ cup chopped green
onions

1 cup chopped black
olives
$1/2$ teaspoon curry powder
1 loaf party rye bread

Combine cheese, mayonnaise, green onions, olives and curry powder in bowl; mix well. Spread on bread slices; place on baking sheet. Broil for 3 to 4 minutes or until bubbly. Serve immediately. Yield: 30 servings.

Approx Per Serving: Cal 128; Prot 3 g; Carbo 8 g; Fiber 1 g;
T Fat 10 g; Chol 10 mg; Sod 240 mg.

 Buy or make canvas shopping bags to bring home groceries from the market.

DEVILED BISCUITS

1 10-count can biscuits   ¼ cup butter
1 4-ounce can deviled   ¼ cup Parmesan cheese
   ham

Cut biscuits into quarters. Place in two 8-inch baking pans. Combine deviled ham and butter in small saucepan. Heat until bubbly, stirring constantly. Pour over biscuits. Sprinkle with cheese. Bake at 400 degrees for 15 minutes or until golden brown. Serve hot. Yield: 40 servings.

Approx Per Serving: Cal 38; Prot 1 g; Carbo 3 g; Fiber 0 g;
    T Fat 3 g; Chol 6 mg; Sod 118 mg.

HAM ROLLS

2 packages party rolls   1 small onion, grated
1 cup margarine, softened   8 ounces sliced cooked
3 tablespoons poppy   ham
   seed   1 cup shredded Swiss
3 tablespoons Dijon   cheese
   mustard   1 cup shredded Cheddar
1 tablespoon   cheese
   Worcestershire sauce

Cut entire packages of rolls into halves horizontally; do not separate rolls. Combine margarine, poppy seed, mustard, Worcestershire sauce and onion in bowl; mix well. Spread over cut surfaces of rolls. Layer ham and cheeses on bottom halves of rolls; replace top halves. Wrap in foil; place on baking sheet. Bake at 400 degrees for 10 to 12 minutes or until heated through. Cool. Cut into individual rolls. Yield: 32 servings.

Approx Per Serving: Cal 184; Prot 6 g; Carbo 15 g; Fiber 1 g;
    T Fat 11 g; Chol 11 mg; Sod 360 mg.

JALAPEÑO PIE

4 jalapeño peppers　　　　6 eggs, beaten
1 pound Cheddar cheese

Chop peppers; shred cheese. Layer peppers and cheese in 8x8-inch baking dish. Pour eggs over cheese. Bake at 350 degrees for 30 minutes or until firm. Cut into 1-inch squares. Serve warm. May substitute chopped ham or pepperoni for peppers. Yield: 64 servings.

Approx Per Serving: Cal 37; Prot 2 g; Carbo <1 g; Fiber <1 g;
　　T Fat 3 g; Chol 27 mg; Sod 51 mg.

BOURSIN MUSHROOMS

16 fresh mushroom caps　　$^1/_4$ cup melted margarine
4 ounces Boursin cheese

Fill mushroom caps with cheese. Place in baking dish. Drizzle with melted margarine. Bake at 350 degrees for 10 to 12 minutes or until cheese melts. Yield: 16 servings.

Approx Per Serving: Cal 83; Prot 1 g; Carbo 2 g; Fiber 1 g;
　　T Fat 8 g; Chol 23 mg; Sod 71 mg.

RANCHO NACHOS

1　8-ounce package　　　6 ounces sharp Cheddar
　tortilla chips　　　　　　cheese, shredded
$^3/_4$ cup ranch salad　　　$^1/_4$ cup sliced green
　dressing　　　　　　　　onions

Arrange chips in shallow baking dish. Drizzle salad dressing over chips. Sprinkle with cheese and green onions. Bake at 350 degrees for 8 minutes or until cheese melts. May also top with sliced black olives, jalapeño peppers or finely chopped green peppers. Yield: 8 servings.

Approx Per Serving: Cal 307; Prot 8 g; Carbo 18 g; Fiber 1 g;
　　T Fat 23 g; Chol 31 mg; Sod 370 mg.

ONION ON RYE ROUNDS

1 loaf party rye bread　　**6 small onions, sliced**
1 cup mayonnaise　　　　**¹/₄ cup Parmesan cheese**

Spread bread slices with mayonnaise. Top each with onion slice. Spread mayonnaise over onion slices; sprinkle with cheese. Place on baking sheet. Broil until golden brown. Serve hot. Yield: 22 servings.

Approx Per Serving: Cal 133; Prot 2 g; Carbo 11 g; Fiber 2 g;
　　T Fat 9 g; Chol 7 mg; Sod 219 mg.

PEPPERONI PIZZA SNACKS

6 English muffins, split　　**8 ounces sliced pepperoni**
1　15-ounce jar pizza　　　**8 ounces mozzarella**
**　sauce**　　　　　　　　　**　cheese, shredded**

Place muffins on baking sheet. Spread with pizza sauce. Top with pepperoni and cheese. Bake at 350 degrees for 12 minutes or until bubbly. Yield: 12 servings.

Approx Per Serving: Cal 256; Prot 12 g; Carbo 20 g; Fiber 1 g;
　　T Fat 13 g; Chol 16 mg; Sod 851 mg.

EASY SAUSAGE BALLS

3 cups baking mix　　　　**1　8-ounce jar Cheez**
¹/₂ cup milk　　　　　　　**　Whiz**
1 pound sausage

Combine baking mix and milk in bowl; mix well. Add sausage and Cheez Whiz; mix well. Drop by spoonfuls onto baking sheet. Bake at 425 degrees for 15 minutes or until brown; drain. Yield: 72 servings.

Approx Per Serving: Cal 47; Prot 1 g; Carbo 4 g; Fiber 0 g;
　　T Fat 3 g; Chol 4 mg; Sod 124 mg.

SHRIMP TIDBITS

1 cup shredded Cheddar
  cheese
1 cup mayonnaise
1 7-ounce can shrimp,
  chopped

3 green onions, chopped
1/2 teaspoon dillweed
Salt to taste
6 English muffins, split

Combine cheese, mayonnaise, shrimp, green onions, dillweed and salt in bowl; mix well. Spread on muffin halves. Cut into quarters; place on rack in broiler pan. Broil 6 inches from heat source for 5 minutes or until cheese melts. May substitute crab meat for shrimp. Yield: 48 servings.

Approx Per Serving: Cal 65; Prot 2 g; Carbo 4 g; Fiber <1 g;
  T Fat 5 g; Chol 12 mg; Sod 95 mg.

SPINACH CHEESE SQUARES

1/4 cup butter
3 eggs, beaten
1 cup flour
1 cup milk
1 teaspoon salt
1 teaspoon baking
  powder

2 10-ounce packages
  frozen chopped
  spinach, thawed,
  drained
16 ounces Monterey Jack
  cheese, shredded

Melt butter in 9x13-inch baking dish. Combine eggs, flour, milk, salt and baking powder in bowl; mix well. Add spinach and cheese; mix well. Spoon into prepared baking dish; do not mix. Bake at 350 degrees for 35 minutes. Let stand for 45 minutes. Cut into bite-sized pieces. May freeze on baking sheet, store in airtight container and reheat at 325 degrees for 12 minutes. Yield: 25 servings.

Approx Per Serving: Cal 124; Prot 7 g; Carbo 6 g; Fiber 1 g;
  T Fat 8 g; Chol 49 mg; Sod 243 mg.

SWEET AND SOUR SMOKIES

1 cup packed brown
  sugar
3 tablespoons flour
1 cup pineapple juice

1/2 cup cider vinegar
2 teaspoons dry mustard
1 1/2 teaspoons soy sauce
2 pounds cocktail franks

Combine brown sugar, flour, pineapple juice, vinegar, dry mustard and soy sauce in saucepan; mix well. Bring to a boil. Add cocktail franks; reduce heat. Simmer for 30 minutes. Serve on toothpicks. Yield: 100 servings.

Approx Per Serving: Cal 40; Prot 2 g; Carbo 3 g; Fiber 2 g;
  T Fat 3 g; Chol 5 mg; Sod 107 mg.
  Nutritional information includes entire amount of sauce.

TACO PIE

8 ounces cream cheese,
  softened
1 cup sour cream
1 envelope taco
  seasoning mix
3 tablespoons picante
  sauce

2 cups shredded lettuce
1 tomato, chopped
1 cup shredded Cheddar
  cheese
1 onion, chopped
1 2-ounce can sliced
  black olives, drained

Combine cream cheese, sour cream, taco mix and picante sauce in bowl; mix well. Spread on round platter. Chill until firm. Layer lettuce, tomato, cheese, onion and olives over chilled mixture. Serve with chips.
Yield: 16 servings.

Approx Per Serving: Cal 132; Prot 4 g; Carbo 5 g; Fiber <1 g;
  T Fat 12 g; Chol 30 mg; Sod 355 mg.

ZUCCHINI APPETIZERS

3 cups thinly sliced
  zucchini
1 cup baking mix
1/2 cup minced onion
2 tablespoons chopped
  parsley

1/2 cup Parmesan cheese
1 clove of garlic, minced
4 eggs, slightly beaten
1/2 cup oil
1/2 teaspoon oregano
Seasoned salt to taste

Combine zucchini, baking mix, onion, parsley, cheese, garlic, eggs, oil, oregano and seasoned salt in bowl; mix well. Spoon into 9x13-inch baking dish. Bake at 350 degrees for 25 to 30 minutes or until golden brown. Cut into 1x2-inch bars. Yield: 48 servings.

Approx Per Serving: Cal 44; Prot 1 g; Carbo 2 g; Fiber <1 g;
  T Fat 3 g; Chol 18 mg; Sod 55 mg.

AVOCADO DIP

1 large avocado, peeled
1/2 cup mayonnaise
1 teaspoon chili sauce
1 clove of garlic, crushed
1 tablespoon lemon juice

2 tablespoons minced
  onion
1 tomato, peeled,
  chopped

Chop avocado coarsely. Combine mayonnaise, chili sauce, garlic, lemon juice, onion and tomato in bowl; mix well. Fold in avocado. Chill until serving time.
Yield: 16 servings.

Approx Per Serving: Cal 71; Prot <1 g; Carbo 2 g; Fiber 1 g;
  T Fat 7 g; Chol 4 mg; Sod 46 mg.

 Choose a clothes washer with adjustable water levels and temperature controls so you can use only as much water and energy as you need.

CARAMEL DIP FOR APPLES

8 ounces cream cheese,
softened
³/₄ cup packed light
brown sugar

¹/₄ cup sugar
1 teaspoon vanilla extract
¹/₂ cup crushed peanuts

Combine all ingredients in bowl; mix well. Chill until serving time. Serve with apple slices. Yield: 12 servings.

Approx Per Serving: Cal 169; Prot 3 g; Carbo 19 g; Fiber 1 g;
T Fat 10 g; Chol 21 mg; Sod 63 mg.

CRAB DIP

1 6-ounce can crab
meat, drained
16 ounces cream cheese,
softened
1 onion, grated

¹/₂ cup mayonnaise
1 cup catsup
2 tablespoons prepared
horseradish
Tabasco sauce to taste

Combine crab meat, cream cheese, onion and mayonnaise in bowl; mix well. Spoon into serving dish. Combine catsup, horseradish and Tabasco sauce in small bowl; mix well. Spoon over crab mixture. Yield: 16 servings.

Approx Per Serving: Cal 181; Prot 5 g; Carbo 6 g; Fiber <1 g;
T Fat 16 g; Chol 45 mg; Sod 338 mg.

DILL DIP

²/₃ cup sour cream
¹/₃ cup mayonnaise
1 tablespoon minced
onion

1 teaspoon parsley flakes
1 tablespoon dillweed
¹/₂ teaspoon seasoned
salt

Combine all ingredients in bowl; mix well. Serve with bite-sized vegetables. Yield: 8 servings.

Approx Per Serving: Cal 106; Prot 1 g; Carbo 1 g; Fiber <1 g;
T Fat 11 g; Chol 14 mg; Sod 195 mg.

ENCHILADA DIP

1/2 envelope enchilada
  seasoning mix
1 cup sour cream
8 ounces cream cheese,
  softened
1   15-ounce can refried
  beans

4 ounces Cheddar
  cheese, shredded
4 ounces Monterey Jack
  cheese, shredded

Combine enchilada mix, sour cream and cream cheese in bowl; mix until smooth. Add beans; mix well. Spoon into lightly greased 7x11-inch baking dish. Sprinkle with cheeses. Bake at 350 degrees for 15 to 20 minutes or until cheese melts. Serve hot or cool with corn chips. Yield: 40 servings.

Approx Per Serving: Cal 68; Prot 2 g; Carbo 4 g; Fiber 2 g;
     T Fat 6 g; Chol 14 mg; Sod 150 mg.

SHRIMP DIP

1 cup sour cream
3 ounces cream cheese,
  softened
1 envelope Italian salad
  dressing mix

2 teaspoons lemon juice
1/2 cup chopped cooked
  shrimp

Cream sour cream and cream cheese in mixer bowl until smooth. Add salad dressing mix and lemon juice; mix well. Fold in shrimp. Chill, covered, for 1 hour or longer. Yield: 12 servings.

Approx Per Serving: Cal 74; Prot 2 g; Carbo 1 g; Fiber <1 g;
     T Fat 7 g; Chol 26 mg; Sod 120 mg.

Speedy
Salads

FROZEN BANANA SALAD

8 ounces cream cheese, softened
1/4 cup milk
2 teaspoons vanilla extract
1/3 cup lemon juice
1 cup confectioners' sugar
16 ounces whipped topping
6 bananas, sliced
2/3 cup chopped pecans

Combine cream cheese, milk, vanilla, lemon juice and confectioners' sugar in mixer bowl; mix until smooth. Fold in whipped topping, bananas and pecans. Spoon into 9x13-inch pan. Freeze until firm. Cut into squares. Yield: 15 servings.

Approx Per Serving: Cal 262; Prot 3 g; Carbo 28 g; Fiber 1 g; T Fat 17 g; Chol 17 mg; Sod 55 mg.

CRANBERRY FLUFF

2 cups cranberries
2 oranges
3/4 cup sugar
2 cups chopped unpeeled apples
1 cup seedless green grape halves
1/2 cup pecans
1 cup whipping cream, whipped

Grind cranberries and oranges in food grinder. Combine with sugar in bowl; mix well. Chill, covered, overnight. Add apples, grapes and pecans; mix well. Fold in whipped cream. Chill until serving time. Yield: 8 servings.

Approx Per Serving: Cal 274; Prot 2 g; Carbo 34 g; Fiber 3 g; T Fat 16 g; Chol 41 mg; Sod 12 mg.

 A refrigerator with a freezer on the top saves 20 percent in energy cost compared to a side-by-side refrigerator/freezer unit.

FIVE-CUP FRUIT SALAD

1 cup mandarin oranges
1 cup pineapple chunks
1 cup coconut

1 cup marshmallows
1 cup sour cream

Combine oranges, pineapple, coconut and marshmallows in bowl; mix well. Fold in sour cream. Chill until serving time. Yield: 6 servings.

Approx Per Serving: Cal 249; Prot 2 g; Carbo 32 g; Fiber 3 g; T Fat 14 g; Chol 17 mg; Sod 73 mg.

HEALTHY FRUIT SALAD

2 pints strawberries, cut into halves
3 cups chopped fresh pineapple
4 bananas, sliced

1 pound seedless grapes, cut into halves
4 containers strawberry low-fat yogurt
1 cup chopped pecans

Alternate layers of strawberries, pineapple, bananas and grapes in large bowl until all fruits are used. Spread with yogurt; sprinkle with pecans. Chill in refrigerator. May toss gently at serving time. Yield: 10 servings.

Approx Per Serving: Cal 255; Prot 5 g; Carbo 42 g; Fiber 3 g; T Fat 10 g; Chol 3 mg; Sod 40 mg.

ORANGE AND CRANBERRY MOLD

1 3-ounce package orange gelatin
1 cup boiling water

1/2 cup orange juice
1 16-ounce can whole cranberry sauce

Dissolve gelatin in boiling water in bowl. Stir in orange juice. Add cranberry sauce; mix well. Pour into mold. Chill until set. Unmold onto serving plate. Yield: 6 servings.

Approx Per Serving: Cal 176; Prot 2 g; Carbo 44 g; Fiber 2 g; T Fat <1 g; Chol 0 mg; Sod 67 mg.

STRAWBERRY SALAD

1 6-ounce package
   strawberry gelatin
1 cup boiling water
2 10-ounce packages
   frozen strawberries,
   thawed

1 8-ounce can crushed
   pineapple, drained
3 bananas, mashed
1 cup chopped pecans
2 cups sour cream

Dissolve gelatin in boiling water in 2-quart bowl. Stir in strawberries, pineapple, bananas and pecans. Pour half the mixture into 9x9-inch dish. Chill until firm. Spread with sour cream. Top with remaining gelatin mixture. Chill until firm. Yield: 12 servings.

Approx Per Serving: Cal 253; Prot 4 g; Carbo 29 g; Fiber 3 g;
    T Fat 15 g; Chol 17 mg; Sod 67 mg.

CHEF'S SALAD

1 head lettuce, torn
1 cup torn spinach
1 cucumber, sliced
6 radishes, sliced
1 tomato, chopped
1/2 cup chopped cooked
   ham

1/4 cup crumbled
   crisp-fried bacon
2 slices American
   cheese, cut into strips
3 slices Swiss cheese,
   cut into strips
2 hard-boiled eggs, sliced

Combine lettuce, spinach, cucumber, radishes and tomato in large salad bowl; toss to mix well. Sprinkle with ham, bacon, cheeses and eggs. Serve with favorite salad dressing. Yield: 6 servings.

Approx Per Serving: Cal 192; Prot 13 g; Carbo 5 g; Fiber 3 g;
    T Fat 13 g; Chol 102 mg; Sod 578 mg.

FRUITED CHICKEN SALAD

3 cups chopped cooked
chicken
1   20-ounce can
pineapple tidbits,
drained
1/4 cup finely chopped
onion

1 cup chopped celery
1 cup green grape halves
1/8 teaspoon seasoned
salt
1 tablespoon lemon juice
1/2 cup toasted almonds
1/2 to 1 cup mayonnaise

Combine chicken, pineapple, onion, celery, grapes, seasoned salt, lemon juice and almonds in bowl; mix well. Add enough mayonnaise to moisten to desired consistency. Chill until serving time. Yield: 8 servings.

Approx Per Serving: Cal 436; Prot 19 g; Carbo 18 g; Fiber 3 g;
T Fat 33 g; Chol 63 mg; Sod 251 mg.

CRAB MEAT SALAD

12 ounces crab meat
1 cucumber, chopped
1 green bell pepper,
chopped

1 medium onion, chopped
1/4 cup mayonnaise
Salt and pepper to taste

Combine crab meat, cucumber, green pepper and onion in salad bowl; toss to mix well. Add mayonnaise, salt and pepper; mix well. Chill, covered, for 1 hour or longer. Serve with crackers. Yield: 4 servings.

Approx Per Serving: Cal 212; Prot 19 g; Carbo 7 g; Fiber 2 g;
T Fat 12 g; Chol 84 mg; Sod 365 mg.

REUBEN SALAD

1 8-ounce can
  sauerkraut
5 slices rye bread
3 tablespoons butter
4 ounces corned beef,
  sliced

8 cups torn leaf lettuce
4 ounces Swiss cheese,
  cubed
3/4 cup Thousand Island
  salad dressing
1/2 teaspoon caraway seed

Rinse and drain sauerkraut. Chill in refrigerator. Trim crusts from bread; cut bread into cubes. Brown in butter in skillet. Cut corned beef into strips. Combine corned beef, sauerkraut, lettuce and cheese in salad bowl. Add salad dressing, bread cubes and caraway seed at serving time; toss to mix well. Yield: 6 servings.

Approx Per Serving: Cal 358; Prot 14 g; Carbo 19 g; Fiber 3 g;
    T Fat 26 g; Chol 57 mg; Sod 909 mg.

SHRIMP AND PASTA SALAD

8 ounces uncooked rotini
3 1/2 pounds cooked
  peeled shrimp
4 stalks celery,
  diagonally sliced
8 black olives, sliced

5 green onions with tops,
  diagonally sliced
2 tablespoons chopped
  parsley
1 8-ounce bottle of
  Italian salad dressing

Cook pasta using package directions. Rinse in cold water and drain. Combine with shrimp, celery, olives, green onions and parsley in airtight container or plastic bag. Add salad dressing; shake gently to coat well. Chill overnight, turning container several times. Yield: 10 servings.

Approx Per Serving: Cal 358; Prot 37 g; Carbo 21 g; Fiber 2 g;
    T Fat 17 g; Chol 310 mg; Sod 510 mg.

TACO SALAD

1 pound lean ground beef
1/4 cup chopped onion
2 tomatoes, chopped
2 teaspoons chili powder
Cumin, salt and pepper
  to taste
1/4 teaspoon garlic powder
1 head lettuce
3 tomatoes, cut into
  wedges
3/4 cup shredded
  Monterey Jack cheese

Brown ground beef with onion in skillet, stirring until ground beef is crumbly; drain. Stir in chopped tomatoes, chili powder, cumin, salt, pepper and garlic powder. Simmer until of desired consistency. Line salad bowl with lettuce. Spoon ground beef mixture over lettuce. Tear remaining lettuce into bite-sized pieces. Place in prepared bowl. Arrange tomato wedges on salad; sprinkle with cheese. Serve immediately. Yield: 6 servings.

Approx Per Serving: Cal 237; Prot 19 g; Carbo 6 g; Fiber 2 g;
  T Fat 15 g; Chol 62 mg; Sod 140 mg.

CRUNCHY TUNA SALAD

1 6-ounce can water-
  pack tuna, drained
1/3 cup chopped sweet
  pickles
1/2 cup sliced celery
1/3 cup chopped pecans
1/2 cup sliced stuffed
  olives
1/4 cup mayonnaise

Combine tuna, pickles, celery, pecans and olives in bowl; mix well. Add mayonnaise; mix well. Spoon onto lettuce-lined salad plates. Garnish with additional olives. Yield: 4 servings.

Approx Per Serving: Cal 264; Prot 14 g; Carbo 10 g; Fiber 2 g;
  T Fat 20 g; Chol 32 mg; Sod 718 mg.

BROCCOLI SALAD

2 bunches broccoli,
   chopped
1 small onion, sliced into
   rings
1/2 cup golden raisins

1/2 cup chopped pecans
3 tablespoons vinegar
3/4 cup mayonnaise
1/3 cup sugar

Combine broccoli, onion, raisins and pecans in bowl; mix well. Combine vinegar, mayonnaise and sugar in small bowl; mix well. Stir into broccoli mixture. Chill for 2 hours or longer. Garnish with crumbled crisp-fried bacon if desired. Yield: 8 servings.

Approx Per Serving: Cal 290; Prot 4 g; Carbo 24 g; Fiber 4 g;
   T Fat 22 g; Chol 12 mg; Sod 143 mg.

CARROT AND RAISIN SALAD

8 carrots, finely shredded
1 cup raisins
1 teaspoon vinegar

1 1/4 cups mayonnaise
3 tablespoons honey
1 teaspoon cinnamon

Combine carrots, raisins and vinegar in bowl; mix well. Combine mayonnaise, honey and cinnamon in small bowl; mix well. Pour over carrots; mix well. Chill, covered, for 2 hours to several days. Yield: 8 servings.

Approx Per Serving: Cal 364; Prot 2 g; Carbo 31 g; Fiber 4 g;
   T Fat 28 g; Chol 20 mg; Sod 223 mg.

For every soft drink bottle you recycle, you save enough energy to run a television set for 1 1/2 hours.

GREEN AND WHITE SALAD

1 10-ounce package
  frozen green peas
1 head cauliflower,
  chopped
1 bunch broccoli,
  chopped
3 small zucchini, sliced
1 cup sliced mushrooms

1 cup chopped pimento
1/2 cup sliced purple
  onion
1 8-ounce bottle of
  creamy cucumber salad
  dressing
Paprika, salt and pepper
  to taste

Thaw peas in cold water in colander; drain. Combine with cauliflower, broccoli, zucchini, mushrooms, pimento and onion in large salad bowl; toss to mix well. Add salad dressing; toss to coat well. Sprinkle with paprika, salt and pepper. Chill for 2 hours or longer. Yield: 12 servings.

Approx Per Serving: Cal 117; Prot 4 g; Carbo 10 g; Fiber 4 g;
  T Fat 8 g; Chol 7 mg; Sod 123 mg.

POTATO SALAD

2 cups refrigerator
  hashed brown potatoes
2 tablespoons
  mayonnaise
2 tablespoons mustard

1/2 cup chopped pickles
2 hard-boiled eggs,
  chopped
Salt and pepper to taste

Cook potatoes in water to cover in saucepan until tender. Drain and cool. Combine with mayonnaise, mustard, pickles, eggs, salt and pepper in bowl; mix well. Chill until serving time. Yield: 4 servings.

Approx Per Serving: Cal 224; Prot 6 g; Carbo 32 g; Fiber 3 g;
  T Fat 9 g; Chol 111 mg; Sod 369 mg.

SEVEN-LAYER SALAD

1 head lettuce, torn
1 8-ounce can sliced
   water chestnuts,
   drained
1 10-ounce package
   frozen peas, thawed,
   drained

1 cup chopped celery
1 cup chopped onion
1 1/2 cups mayonnaise
2 tablespoons sugar
2 cups shredded
   Cheddar cheese
1 cup real bacon bits

Layer lettuce, water chestnuts, peas, celery and onion in large glass bowl. Spread mayonnaise over top, sealing to edge. Sprinkle with sugar, cheese and bacon. Chill, covered, for 24 hours. Yield: 10 servings.

Approx Per Serving: Cal 419; Prot 10 g; Carbo 13 g; Fiber 3 g; T Fat 37 g; Chol 49 mg; Sod 483 mg.

APPLE SLAW

4 1/2 cups thinly sliced red
   apples
3 cups finely shredded
   cabbage
1 cup sour cream

3 tablespoons lemon juice
1 tablespoon sugar
1 tablespoon poppy seed
Salt and pepper to taste

Combine apples and cabbage in salad bowl; mix well. Combine sour cream, lemon juice, sugar, poppy seed, salt and pepper in small bowl; mix well. Add to slaw; toss lightly to mix well. Chill for 1 hour or longer. May substitute yogurt for sour cream. Yield: 8 servings.

Approx Per Serving: Cal 111; Prot 1 g; Carbo 14 g; Fiber 2 g; T Fat 6 g; Chol 13 mg; Sod 20 mg.

A Month of

Main Dishes

BEST EASY BEEF STEW

2 pounds beef round
  steak, cubed
1 7-ounce can
  mushrooms, drained
1 envelope onion soup
  mix

1 10-ounce can cream
  of mushroom soup
4 carrots, cut into 2-inch
  pieces
8 new potatoes, peeled

Layer beef cubes and mushrooms in large baking dish. Sprinkle soup mix over mushrooms. Spoon mushroom soup on top. Arrange carrots and potatoes around edge of dish. Bake, tightly covered, at 300 degrees for 3 hours. Yield: 4 servings.

Approx Per Serving: Cal 460; Prot 46 g; Carbo 26 g; Fiber 4 g;
    T Fat 19 g; Chol 128 mg; Sod 1178 mg.

STUFFED MINUTE STEAKS

2 cups dry stuffing mix
1 green bell pepper,
  chopped
1 cup hot water
2 tablespoons margarine

4 4-ounce beef minute
  steaks
1/4 cup honey
2 tablespoons soy sauce

Combine stuffing mix and green pepper in bowl. Add mixture of hot water and margarine; mix well. Spoon 1/2 cup stuffing mixture onto each steak. Roll to enclose filling; secure with toothpicks. Place in shallow baking pan. Pour mixture of honey and soy sauce over top. Bake at 375 degrees for 20 minutes. Yield: 4 servings.

Approx Per Serving: Cal 386; Prot 24 g; Carbo 45 g; Fiber <1 g;
    T Fat 13 g; Chol 55 mg; Sod 1092 mg.

SLOW-COOKER ROAST BEEF

1   3-pound sirloin tip
  roast
1/2 cup flour
1 envelope onion soup
  mix

1 envelope brown gravy
  mix
2 cups ginger ale

Coat roast with flour. Place in slow-cooker. Combine soup mix, gravy mix, remaining flour and ginger ale in bowl; mix well. Pour over roast. Cook on Low for 8 to 10 hours or until roast is tender. Yield: 6 servings.

Approx Per Serving: Cal 381; Prot 44 g; Carbo 18 g; Fiber <1 g;
  T Fat 13 g; Chol 128 mg; Sod 382 mg.

BEEF AND BROCCOLI STIR-FRY

1 pound boneless beef
  sirloin
1 tablespoon cornstarch
1 tablespoon soy sauce
1 clove of garlic, minced
1/4 teaspoon salt

2 tablespoons oil
2 cups broccoli flowerets
1   2-ounce can
  mushrooms
1/3 cup chicken broth

Slice sirloin into thin strips. Combine with cornstarch and soy sauce in bowl; mix well. Stir-fry garlic with salt in oil in skillet or wok. Add beef. Stir-fry for several minutes. Remove beef; set aside. Add broccoli, undrained mushrooms and broth. Bring to a boil; reduce heat. Cook, covered, for 2 minutes. Add beef. Heat to serving temperature. Serve immediately with rice. Yield: 4 servings.

Approx Per Serving: Cal 238; Prot 23 g; Carbo 5 g; Fiber 2 g;
  T Fat 14 g; Chol 64 mg; Sod 562 mg.

CHOP CHOP SUEY

1 pound ground beef
1/4 cup chopped onion
1 3/4 cups beef broth
1 tablespoon soy sauce
1 1/2 teaspoons sugar

1 package frozen
Chinese vegetables
with sauce
1 1/3 cups uncooked
minute rice

Brown ground beef with onion in large skillet, stirring until ground beef is crumbly; drain well. Add broth, soy sauce, sugar and vegetables. Simmer, covered, for 2 minutes. Stir in uncooked rice. Cover; remove from heat. Let stand for 5 minutes. Serve with chow mein noodles. Yield: 4 servings.

Approx Per Serving: Cal 368; Prot 23 g; Carbo 40 g; Fiber 4 g;
    T Fat 13 g; Chol 59 mg; Sod 681 mg.
    Nutritional information does not include sauce from frozen Chinese vegetables.

YORKSHIRE MEATBALLS

1 1/2 pounds ground beef
1 envelope onion soup
  mix
1/4 cup chili sauce
1 egg
1 1/2 cups sifted flour

1 1/2 teaspoons baking
  powder
4 eggs, beaten
1 1/2 cups milk
3 tablespoons melted
  margarine

Combine ground beef, soup mix, chili sauce and 1 egg in bowl; mix well. Shape into small meatballs. Place in greased 9x13-inch baking dish. Sift flour and baking powder into bowl. Add mixture of 4 eggs, milk and margarine; beat until blended. Pour over meatballs. Bake at 350 degrees for 50 minutes or until golden. Yield: 8 servings.

Approx Per Serving: Cal 342; Prot 20 g; Carbo 22 g; Fiber 1 g;
    T Fat 19 g; Chol 183 mg; Sod 405 mg.

To save energy let leftovers cool before putting them away.

MINI MEAT LOAVES WITH VEGETABLES

1½ pounds ground beef
1 egg
1 8-ounce can tomato
  sauce
Italian seasoning to taste
1 3-ounce can French-
  fried onions

6 small potatoes, thinly
  sliced
1 16-ounce package
  frozen mixed broccoli,
  corn and red pepper,
  thawed, drained

Mix ground beef, egg and half the tomato sauce in bowl. Add Italian seasoning and half the French-fried onions; mix well. Shape into 4 loaves. Place in 9x13-inch baking dish. Arrange potatoes around loaves. Bake, covered, at 375 degrees for 35 minutes. Spoon broccoli mixture around loaves. Spoon remaining tomato sauce over loaves. Bake, uncovered, for 15 minutes. Sprinkle with remaining French-fried onions. Bake for 5 minutes longer. Yield: 4 servings.

Approx Per Serving: Cal 600; Prot 35 g; Carbo 64 g; Fiber 8 g;
   T Fat 25 g; Chol 148 mg; Sod 499 mg.

MEXICAN CORN BREAD BAKE

2 pounds ground beef
1 onion, chopped
1 green bell pepper,
  chopped
1 teaspoon salt
1 envelope chili
  seasoning mix

1 8-ounce can tomato
  sauce
1 7-ounce package corn
  muffin mix
1 cup evaporated milk
1 cup shredded sharp
  Cheddar cheese

Brown ground beef in skillet; drain. Add onion and green pepper. Cook for several minutes, stirring frequently. Add salt, seasoning mix and tomato sauce. Spoon into baking dish. Spread mixture of corn muffin mix and evaporated milk over top. Sprinkle with cheese. Bake at 400 degrees for 20 minutes or until golden brown. Yield: 6 servings.

Approx Per Serving: Cal 529; Prot 38 g; Carbo 22 g; Fiber 1 g;
   T Fat 32 g; Chol 131 mg; Sod 998 mg.

MEAL-IN-A-LOAF

1 pound ground beef
1/2 cup chopped green
bell pepper
1/2 cup chopped celery
1/2 teaspoon pepper
1 tablespoon
Worcestershire sauce

1 teaspoon salt
1 10-ounce can Cheddar
cheese soup
1 16-ounce loaf unsliced
French bread
4 ounces Cheddar
cheese, sliced

Brown ground beef in skillet; drain. Add next 6 ingredients; mix well. Simmer for 5 minutes. Cut off top of loaf. Scoop out loaf to form shell, reserving bread. Crumble enough reserved bread to measure 2 cups. Add to ground beef mixture. Spoon into bread shell. Top with cheese slices; replace top of loaf. Place on baking sheet. Bake at 350 degrees for 8 minutes or until heated through. Yield: 5 servings.

Approx Per Serving: Cal 671; Prot 39 g; Carbo 52 g; Fiber 2 g;
T Fat 33 g; Chol 116 mg; Sod 1627 mg.

ZUCCHINI AND GROUND BEEF CASSEROLE

6 cups sliced zucchini
1/4 cup chopped onion
1 pound ground beef
1 tablespoon butter
1 package Stove Top
stuffing mix

1 1/2 cups water
1 10-ounce can cream
of chicken soup
1 cup sour cream
1 cup shredded carrots

Cook zucchini in a small amount of water in saucepan for 3 minutes; drain well. Brown onion and ground beef in butter in skillet; drain. Mix stuffing mix with water. Spoon half the mixture into greased 9x13-inch baking dish. Combine soup and sour cream in bowl. Add zucchini, ground beef and carrots. Layer ground beef mixture and remaining stuffing in prepared dish. Bake at 350 degrees for 40 minutes or until brown. Yield: 6 servings.

Approx Per Serving: Cal 369; Prot 20 g; Carbo 20 g; Fiber 2 g;
T Fat 24 g; Chol 75 mg; Sod 616 mg.

HAM AND BROCCOLI STRATA

12 slices white bread,
    crusts trimmed
12 ounces American
    cheese, sliced
1 10-ounce package
    frozen broccoli, thawed
2 cups chopped cooked
    ham

6 eggs
3¹/2 cups milk
2 tablespoons chopped
    onion
1/2 teaspoon salt
1/4 teaspoon dry mustard

Layer 6 slices bread, cheese, broccoli and ham in lightly greased 9x13-inch baking pan. Place remaining bread on top. Pour mixture of eggs, milk, onion, salt and dry mustard over layers. Let stand, covered, in refrigerator for 6 hours to overnight. Bake at 325 degrees for 45 to 55 minutes or until set and light brown. Let stand for 10 minutes before serving. Yield: 8 servings.

Approx Per Serving: Cal 462; Prot 31 g; Carbo 29 g; Fiber 2 g;
    T Fat 25 g; Chol 234 mg; Sod 1527 mg.

HAM AND CHEESE QUICHE

3 eggs, beaten
3/4 cup milk
1/2 teaspoon salt
Pepper to taste
1 cup shredded sharp
    Cheddar cheese

1 cup chopped cooked
    ham
1 unbaked 9-inch pie shell

Beat eggs with milk, salt and pepper in bowl. Add cheese and ham. Pour into pie shell. Bake at 350 degrees for 45 minutes or until set. Let stand for several minutes before serving. Yield: 6 servings.

Approx Per Serving: Cal 321; Prot 16 g; Carbo 15 g; Fiber 1 g;
    T Fat 21 g; Chol 143 mg; Sod 835 mg.

GLAZED HAM STEAKS

1/4 cup prepared mustard
1/2 cup packed light
  brown sugar
1/8 teaspoon cloves
2 tablespoons pineapple
  juice

6 1/2-inch thick 4-ounce
   ham steaks
1 20-ounce can
   pineapple slices,
   drained

Combine mustard, brown sugar, cloves and pineapple juice in bowl; mix well. Place ham steaks in baking dish. Brush with mustard mixture. Broil for 4 minutes or until light brown. Turn ham steaks over. Brush with remaining mustard mixture. Arrange 2 pineapple slices on each steak. Broil for several minutes longer or until light brown. May also grill for 6 minutes on each side. Yield: 6 servings.

Approx Per Serving: Cal 246; Prot 20 g; Carbo 32 g; Fiber 1 g;
  T Fat 5 g; Chol 42 mg; Sod 1144 mg.

BAKED HAM WITH HORSERADISH GLAZE

1 5-pound fully cooked
   or canned ham
1 cup packed light brown
  sugar

Whole cloves to taste
1/3 cup prepared
  horseradish
1/4 cup lemon juice

Place ham in baking dish. Bake at 325 degrees using package directions or for about 1 1/2 hours. Remove from oven. Combine brown sugar, cloves, horseradish and lemon juice in saucepan. Bring to a boil. Pour over ham. Bake at 400 degrees for 15 minutes, basting occasionally. Yield: 8 servings.

Approx Per Serving: Cal 552; Prot 71 g; Carbo 28 g; Fiber <1 g;
  T Fat 16 g; Chol 156 mg; Sod 3784 mg.

EASY ITALIAN PORK DINNER

4 4-ounce pork chops
1/4 cup Italian salad
  dressing
2 tablespoons oil
4 medium potatoes,
  peeled, thinly sliced
1 small onion, sliced
2 tablespoons butter
2 tablespoons Italian
  salad dressing
1/4 cup shredded
  mozzarella cheese

Marinate pork chops in 1/4 cup salad dressing in baking dish for 3 hours. Brown in oil in skillet. Return to marinade. Layer potatoes and onion over chops. Dot with butter. Drizzle with 2 tablespoons salad dressing. Sprinkle with cheese. Bake, covered, at 375 degrees for 1 hour or until tender. Yield: 4 servings.

Approx Per Serving: Cal 551; Prot 27 g; Carbo 38 g; Fiber 3 g;
  T Fat 35 g; Chol 90 mg; Sod 246 mg.

PORK CHOP AND HASHED BROWN CASSEROLE

1 10-ounce can cream
  of mushroom soup
1/2 cup milk
1/2 cup sour cream
1/2 teaspoon salt
1 cup shredded Cheddar
  cheese
1 24-ounce package
  frozen hashed brown
  potatoes, thawed
1 3-ounce can French-
  fried onions
6 3-ounce pork chops
1 tablespoon oil

Combine first 4 ingredients in bowl; mix well. Add half the cheese, potatoes and half the French-fried onions; mix well. Spoon into 9x13-inch baking dish. Brown pork chops in oil in skillet. Arrange over potato mixture. Bake, covered, at 350 degrees for 40 minutes. Top with remaining cheese and French-fried onions. Bake, uncovered, for 5 minutes longer. Yield: 6 servings.

Approx Per Serving: Cal 599; Prot 28 g; Carbo 42 g; Fiber 3 g;
  T Fat 37 g; Chol 84 mg; Sod 780 mg.

PORK CHOP AND RICE BAKE

6 3-ounce pork chops
2 tablespoons margarine
1 cup uncooked rice
1 envelope onion soup
  mix

1 4-ounce can sliced
  mushrooms, drained
3 cups hot water
1/4 cup chopped green
  onions

Brown pork chops in margarine in skillet. Layer uncooked rice, soup mix and mushrooms in 9x13-inch baking dish. Pour hot water over rice. Arrange pork chops on top. Sprinkle with green onions. Bake, covered, at 350 degrees for 45 minutes. Bake, uncovered, for 10 minutes. Yield: 6 servings.

Approx Per Serving: Cal 275; Prot 20 g; Carbo 27 g; Fiber 1 g;
    T Fat 10 g; Chol 52 mg; Sod 272 mg.

SWEET AND SOUR KIELBASA

2 pounds kielbasa
  sausage
1 20-ounce can
  pineapple chunks
1 10-ounce jar red
  currant jelly
1 teaspoon ginger
1 tablespoon vinegar

1 tablespoon honey
1 tablespoon dry mustard
2 tablespoons cornstarch
2 tablespoons water
1 green bell pepper,
  sliced
1 red bell pepper, sliced

Place kielbasa in baking dish. Bake at 375 degrees for 20 minutes. Cut into 1/2-inch slices. Drain pineapple, reserving juice. Combine juice, jelly, ginger, vinegar, honey and dry mustard in saucepan. Heat until jelly melts. Stir in mixture of cornstarch and water. Cook until thickened, stirring constantly. Add kielbasa and peppers. Cook over low heat for 15 minutes. Add pineapple. Cook until heated through. Yield: 6 servings.

Approx Per Serving: Cal 452; Prot 10 g; Carbo 61 g; Fiber 2 g;
    T Fat 20 g; Chol 47 mg; Sod 778 mg.

ONE-POT CHICKEN TETRAZZINI

3 tablespoons melted
   margarine
1/4 teaspoon onion
   powder
2 cups chopped cooked
   chicken
6 ounces uncooked
   spaghetti, broken

1 10-ounce can cream
   of chicken soup
21/2 cups chicken broth
1 teaspoon lemon juice
Nutmeg to taste
1/4 teaspoon pepper
1 4-ounce can sliced
   mushrooms, drained

Blend margarine and onion powder in saucepan. Stir in chicken and uncooked spaghetti. Add mixture of soup, broth, lemon juice, nutmeg and pepper; mix well. Sprinkle mushrooms on top; cover. Bring to a boil; reduce heat. Simmer for 15 minutes or until spaghetti is tender, stirring occasionally. Yield: 6 servings.

Approx Per Serving: Cal 309; Prot 21 g; Carbo 26 g; Fiber 2 g; T Fat 13 g; Chol 46 mg; Sod 883 mg.

CHICKEN AND RICE CASSEROLE

3 slices bacon
11/2 cups uncooked rice
1 envelope onion soup
   mix
1 10-ounce can cream
   of mushroom soup
11/2 cups water

1 3-pound chicken,
   cut up
1 4-ounce can
   mushrooms, drained
2 tablespoons chopped
   pimento

Cut bacon slices in halves. Layer bacon and uncooked rice in 9x13-inch baking dish. Combine soup mix, soup and water in bowl; mix well. Pour half the mixture over rice. Rinse chicken and pat dry. Arrange in dish. Layer mushrooms and remaining soup mixture on top. Sprinkle with pimento. Bake, covered, at 350 degrees for 11/2 hours or until chicken is tender. Yield: 4 servings.

Approx Per Serving: Cal 688; Prot 57 g; Carbo 64 g; Fiber 2 g; T Fat 21 g; Chol 157 mg; Sod 1076 mg.

SOUR CREAM CHICKEN BREASTS

¹/₂ cup sour cream
¹/₂ cup mayonnaise
1 tablespoon Parmesan
  cheese
1 teaspoon soy sauce

¹/₂ teaspoon dry mustard
6 4-ounce chicken
  breast filets
¹/₂ cup fine dry bread
  crumbs

Combine sour cream, mayonnaise, cheese, soy sauce and dry mustard in bowl; mix well. Rinse chicken. Dip in mayonnaise mixture; coat with crumbs. Place in baking dish. Bake at 350 degrees for 1 hour or until chicken is tender. Yield: 6 servings.

Approx Per Serving: Cal 302; Prot 22 g; Carbo 8 g; Fiber <1 g;
  T Fat 20 g; Chol 69 mg; Sod 303 mg.

HAWAIIAN CHICKEN

8 chicken breast quarters
¹/₄ cup prepared mustard
¹/₄ cup molasses
¹/₄ cup vinegar

2 tablespoons soy sauce
¹/₂ cup crushed pineapple
¹/₄ cup packed light
  brown sugar

Rinse chicken and pat dry. Arrange in baking dish. Combine mustard, molasses, vinegar, soy sauce, pineapple and brown sugar in dish; mix well. Spoon over chicken. Bake at 325 degrees for 1 hour or until chicken is tender, basting frequently. Yield: 8 servings.

Approx Per Serving: Cal 161; Prot 20 g; Carbo 17 g; Fiber <1 g;
  T Fat 1 g; Chol 49 mg; Sod 423 mg.

 If you recycle a 12-inch stack of newspapers, you save enough energy to take a hot shower every day for a week.

DEEP-DISH CHICKEN PIE

1 10-ounce can cream
   of celery soup
1/2 cup milk
1 5-ounce can chicken
1/2 cup frozen peas

1 tablespoon chopped
  onion
Pepper to taste
1 cup baking mix
1/3 cup milk

Combine soup and 1/2 cup milk in bowl. Add chicken, peas, onion and pepper; mix well. Spoon into baking dish. Combine baking mix and 1/3 cup milk in bowl. Drop by spoonfuls over chicken mixture. Bake at 450 degrees for 20 minutes or until biscuits are brown. Yield: 4 servings.

Approx Per Serving: Cal 295; Prot 16 g; Carbo 31 g; Fiber 1 g;
   T Fat 12 g; Chol 44 mg; Sod 999 mg.

CHICKEN CREOLE

4 4-ounce chicken
   breast filets
3 tablespoons butter
1 green bell pepper,
   chopped
1 onion, sliced

1 cup sliced celery
1 16-ounce can
   tomatoes, chopped
1/4 cup steak sauce
1/2 teaspoon salt
1/8 teaspoon pepper

Rinse chicken and pat dry. Brown in butter in skillet; remove to warm platter. Sauté green pepper, onion and celery in pan drippings until tender-crisp. Add chicken, tomatoes, steak sauce, salt and pepper; mix well. Simmer, covered, for 15 minutes or until chicken is tender. Serve over hot cooked rice. Yield: 4 servings.

Approx Per Serving: Cal 228; Prot 22 g; Carbo 13 g; Fiber 3 g;
   T Fat 10 g; Chol 72 mg; Sod 753 mg.

CRESCENT ROLL-UPS

1 8-count can crescent rolls
2 cups chopped cooked turkey
1 10-ounce can cream of chicken soup
1 10-ounce can Cheddar cheese soup
1 cup sour cream
2 cups shredded Cheddar cheese

Separate crescent rolls. Spoon 1/4 cup turkey onto each roll. Roll into crescents. Place in 9x13-inch baking dish. Pour mixture of soups and sour cream over top. Sprinkle with cheese. Bake at 350 degrees for 20 to 30 minutes or until light brown. Yield: 4 servings.

Approx Per Serving: Cal 821; Prot 44 g; Carbo 36 g; Fiber <1 g; T Fat 55 g; Chol 160 mg; Sod 1977 mg.

ONE-DISH TURKEY DINNER

1 8-ounce package corn bread stuffing mix
8 2-ounce slices deli turkey breast or turkey breast luncheon meat
1 10-ounce can cream of mushroom soup
1 cup evaporated milk
1 10-ounce package frozen broccoli
1 cup shredded Cheddar cheese
1 cup crushed butter crackers

Prepare stuffing mix using package directions. Spoon stuffing onto turkey slices; roll up to enclose filling. Place in greased 8x8-inch baking dish. Pour mixture of soup and evaporated milk over rolls. Cook broccoli for half the time suggested in package directions; drain. Arrange over rolls. Sprinkle with cheese and cracker crumbs. Bake at 350 degrees for 30 to 40 minutes or until cheese melts. Yield: 8 servings.

Approx Per Serving: Cal 349; Prot 27 g; Carbo 27 g; Fiber 2 g; T Fat 16 g; Chol 64 mg; Sod 835 mg.

RED CLAM SPAGHETTI

2 cloves of garlic, minced
3 tablespoons olive oil
1 tablespoon flour
1 6-ounce can minced
  clams
1 20-ounce can Italian
  tomatoes, mashed

2 tablespoons parsley
  flakes
1 16-ounce package
  spaghetti

Sauté garlic in olive oil in skillet. Stir in flour. Cook for 1 minute. Add undrained clams, tomatoes and parsley flakes. Simmer for 15 minutes. Cook spaghetti using package directions. Serve with clam sauce. Yield: 6 servings.

Approx Per Serving: Cal 406; Prot 18 g; Carbo 64 g; Fiber 4 g; T Fat 8 g; Chol 19 mg; Sod 187 mg.

BLEU CHEESE FISH FILETS

4 4-ounce fish filets
1 small onion, chopped
3 tablespoons butter
1/4 cup flour
1/4 teaspoon salt

1/2 teaspoon celery salt
2 cups milk
1/4 cup sliced green olives
1/2 cup crumbled bleu
  cheese

Arrange fish filets in greased 9x13-inch baking dish. Sauté onion in butter in skillet. Stir in flour, salt and celery salt. Add milk. Cook until thickened, stirring constantly; remove from heat. Stir in olives and bleu cheese. Pour over fish. Bake at 350 degrees for 25 to 30 minutes or until fish flakes easily. Serve with rice. Yield: 4 servings.

Approx Per Serving: Cal 400; Prot 32 g; Carbo 14 g; Fiber 1 g; T Fat 24 g; Chol 107 mg; Sod 1132 mg.

 Run your dishwasher only with full loads.

PARMESAN-BAKED ORANGE ROUGHY

1 egg
1/4 cup milk
1 cup butter cracker
  crumbs
1/3 cup Parmesan cheese
1/8 teaspoon pepper

1 pound ocean perch
  filets
1/3 cup melted butter
1 tablespoon lemon juice
1/3 cup margarine

Beat egg and milk in bowl. Combine crumbs, cheese and pepper in shallow dish. Coat filets with crumb mixture, egg mixture and crumb mixture. Place in melted butter in 9x13-inch baking pan, turning to coat both sides. Bake at 425 degrees for 15 to 20 minutes or until fish flakes easily. Combine lemon juice and margarine in small saucepan. Heat until margarine is melted. Serve over fish. Yield: 4 servings.

Approx Per Serving: Cal 519; Prot 24 g; Carbo 17 g; Fiber <1 g;
  T Fat 42 g; Chol 140 mg; Sod 730 mg.

SHRIMP AND BROCCOLI LINGUINE

1 16-ounce package
  linguine
1 clove of garlic, minced
1/2 cup butter
3/4 cup olive oil

Flowerets of 1 bunch
  broccoli
1 10-ounce package
  frozen cooked shrimp

Cook linguine using package directions. Keep warm. Sauté garlic in butter in skillet. Add olive oil. Heat for 30 seconds. Add broccoli. Stir-fry for several minutes. Add shrimp. Stir-fry for 2 minutes or until heated through. Serve over hot linguine. Yield: 6 servings.

Approx Per Serving: Cal 670; Prot 11 g; Carbo 60 g; Fiber 5 g;
  T Fat 43 g; Chol 41 mg; Sod 147 mg.

No-Fuss
Vegetables
& Side Dishes

BAKED ASPARAGUS

5 slices bread, cubed
1 16-ounce can
   asparagus, drained
3 eggs, beaten

2 cups milk
Salt and pepper to taste
1 cup shredded Cheddar
   cheese

Layer bread and asparagus in buttered baking dish. Beat eggs with milk, salt and pepper in bowl. Pour over asparagus. Top with cheese. Bake at 325 degrees for 1 hour. Yield: 4 servings.

Approx Per Serving: Cal 357; Prot 21 g; Carbo 26 g; Fiber 2 g;
    T Fat 20 g; Chol 206 mg; Sod 724 mg.

GREEN BEANS WITH ALMONDS

4 cups cut fresh green
   beans
¼ cup sliced celery

2 tablespoons slivered
   almonds
2 tablespoons margarine

Cook beans in a small amount of water in saucepan until tender; drain. Sauté celery and almonds in margarine in skillet. Add beans; mix gently. Yield: 4 servings.

Approx Per Serving: Cal 121; Prot 3 g; Carbo 11 g; Fiber 4 g;
    T Fat 8 g; Chol 0 mg; Sod 78 mg.

PARTY LIMA BEANS

3 10-ounce packages
   frozen lima beans
¾ cup margarine
1 tablespoon dry mustard

¾ cup packed brown
   sugar
1 tablespoon molasses
1 cup sour cream

Cook beans using package directions; drain. Stir in margarine. Sprinkle with mixture of dry mustard and brown sugar. Stir in molasses and sour cream. Spoon into baking dish. Bake at 350 degrees for 45 minutes. Yield: 8 servings.

Approx Per Serving: Cal 408; Prot 8 g; Carbo 43 g; Fiber 9 g;
    T Fat 23 g; Chol 13 mg; Sod 258 mg.

LEMON AND GARLIC BROCCOLI

1 bunch fresh broccoli
1 clove of garlic, minced
2 tablespoons olive oil

Juice of 1/2 lemon
Salt and pepper to taste
1/4 cup Parmesan cheese

Separate broccoli into flowerets; slice stems. Cook in water in saucepan for 8 minutes or until tender; drain. Sauté garlic in olive oil in skillet for 2 minutes. Add broccoli; toss to coat well. Stir in lemon juice, salt and pepper. Spoon into serving dish. Sprinkle with Parmesan cheese. Yield: 4 servings.

Approx Per Serving: Cal 109; Prot 5 g; Carbo 6 g; Fiber 3 g; T Fat 9 g; Chol 4 mg; Sod 118 mg.

BROCCOLI CASSEROLE

2 10-ounce packages
   frozen chopped broccoli
4 ounces Velveeta
   cheese, chopped

1 1/2 cups butter cracker
   crumbs
1 tablespoon margarine

Cook broccoli using package directions; drain. Stir in cheese until melted; remove from heat. Add 1 cup cracker crumbs; mix well. Spoon into greased 1 1/2-quart baking dish. Top with remaining 1/2 cup cracker crumbs; dot with margarine. Bake at 350 degrees for 20 minutes. Yield: 6 servings.

Approx Per Serving: Cal 219; Prot 9 g; Carbo 20 g; Fiber 3 g; T Fat 15 g; Chol 18 mg; Sod 525 mg.

 You can lower the baking temperature by 25 degrees if you use glass or ceramic baking dishes since these materials retain heat better.

TWO-CHEESE BROCCOLI

Flowerets of 1 pound
  broccoli
1 medium onion, cut into
  quarters
1/4 cup butter
2 tablespoons flour

1 cup milk
3 ounces cream cheese,
  softened
2 ounces sharp Cheddar
  cheese, shredded

Steam broccoli and onion over boiling water until tender-crisp. Melt butter in saucepan. Stir in flour. Add milk gradually. Cook until thickened, stirring constantly. Add cream cheese; mix until smooth. Add broccoli and onion; mix gently. Spoon into 1 1/2-quart baking dish. Top with Cheddar cheese. Bake, covered, at 350 degrees for 30 minutes. Yield: 4 servings.

Approx Per Serving: Cal 310; Prot 9 g; Carbo 12 g; Fiber 2 g;
  T Fat 26 g; Chol 77 mg; Sod 286 mg.

SWEET AND SOUR BRUSSELS SPROUTS

1 10-ounce package
  frozen Brussels sprouts
2 tablespoons oil
1/4 cup vinegar
1 tablespoon sugar

1/2 teaspoon salt
Pepper to taste
2 tablespoons Parmesan
  cheese

Cook Brussels sprouts using package directions; drain. Place in baking dish. Combine oil, vinegar, sugar, salt and pepper in small bowl; mix well. Pour over Brussels sprouts. Sprinkle with cheese. Bake, covered, at 350 degrees for 15 minutes or until heated through. May use 1 pint fresh Brussels sprouts if preferred. Yield: 4 servings.

Approx Per Serving: Cal 116; Prot 4 g; Carbo 10 g; Fiber 3 g;
  T Fat 8 g; Chol 2 mg; Sod 330 mg.

BAKED CABBAGE

1 head cabbage, cut into
  8 wedges
1 cup water
2 tablespoons flour
2 tablespoons sugar

Salt and pepper to taste
3 tablespoons margarine
1 cup hot milk
1 cup shredded Cheddar
  cheese

Cook cabbage, covered, in water in saucepan for 10 minutes; drain well. Place in 8x12-inch baking dish. Sprinkle with mixture of flour, sugar, salt and pepper; dot with margarine. Pour heated milk over top. Top with cheese. Bake at 350 degrees for 35 minutes. Yield: 8 servings.

Approx Per Serving: Cal 141; Prot 5 g; Carbo 8 g; Fiber 1 g;
  T Fat 10 g; Chol 19 mg; Sod 157 mg.

RED CABBAGE SKILLET

1 large onion, finely
  chopped
2 tablespoons shortening
2 apples, peeled, thinly
  sliced
1 cup water
1/2 cup red wine vinegar

2 tablespoons sugar
1 teaspoon salt
Pepper to taste
1 bay leaf
1 medium head red
  cabbage, shredded
1 tablespoon flour

Sauté onion in shortening in large skillet for 3 to 4 minutes. Add apples. Cook for several minutes. Stir in water, vinegar, sugar, salt, pepper and bay leaf. Bring to a boil. Add cabbage. Simmer, tightly covered, for 40 to 45 minutes or until cabbage is tender, stirring occasionally. Remove bay leaf. Stir in flour just before serving. Cook until thickened, stirring constantly. Yield: 8 servings.

Approx Per Serving: Cal 81; Prot 1 g; Carbo 13 g; Fiber 2 g;
  T Fat 3 g; Chol 0 mg; Sod 273 mg.

DILLED CARROTS

8 carrots
1 cup chopped onion
1 clove of garlic, minced
2 tablespoons oil
1 tablespoon flour
1 cup milk

1 10-ounce can cream
    of celery soup
1/2 teaspoon dillseed
1 teaspoon sugar
Garlic powder, salt and
    pepper to taste

Peel carrots and cut into julienne strips. Sauté carrots, onion and garlic in oil in saucepan for 5 minutes. Sprinkle with flour. Stir in milk and soup. Add dillseed and sugar. Simmer until carrots are tender. Season with garlic powder, salt and pepper. Yield: 6 servings.

Approx Per Serving: Cal 158; Prot 3 g; Carbo 19 g; Fiber 4 g;
    T Fat 8 g; Chol 11 mg; Sod 408 mg.

CORN PUDDING

1 17-ounce can
    cream-style corn
1/4 cup flour
1/4 cup sugar

3/4 cup milk
3 eggs
1/4 cup melted margarine
Salt and pepper to taste

Combine corn, flour, sugar, milk, eggs, margarine, salt and pepper in bowl; mix well. Spoon into greased 1 1/2-quart baking dish. Bake at 375 degrees for 45 minutes or until set. Yield: 6 servings.

Approx Per Serving: Cal 236; Prot 6 g; Carbo 29 g; Fiber 2 g;
    T Fat 12 g; Chol 111 mg; Sod 366 mg.

Convection ovens are 30 percent faster than standard models and more energy-efficient.

EGGPLANT CASSEROLE

1 medium eggplant
1/2 cup milk
2 tablespoons melted
  margarine
1 small onion, chopped

1 green bell pepper,
  finely chopped
1 egg, beaten
1 cup bread crumbs

Peel eggplant and cut into cubes. Cook in water to cover in saucepan for 8 minutes; drain. Add margarine, onion, green pepper, egg and bread crumbs; mix well. Spoon into baking dish. Bake at 350 degrees for 30 minutes. Yield: 6 servings.

Approx Per Serving: Cal 153; Prot 5 g; Carbo 20 g; Fiber 4 g;
    T Fat 6 g; Chol 39 mg; Sod 191 mg.

MARINATED OKRA

2 pounds small tender
  okra
1 tablespoon vinegar
1 8-ounce bottle of
  Italian salad dressing
Salt and pepper to taste

1 small onion, finely
  chopped
1 green bell pepper,
  finely chopped
1 tablespoon chopped
  parsley

Bring okra, vinegar and water to cover to a boil in large saucepan. Cook just until tender, stirring occasionally; do not overcook. Rinse in cold water. Combine salad dressing, salt, pepper, onion, green pepper and parsley in bowl; mix well. Add okra; mix gently. Marinate in refrigerator for several hours to overnight. Yield: 8 servings.

Approx Per Serving: Cal 177; Prot 3 g; Carbo 13 g; Fiber 3 g;
    T Fat 17 g; Chol 0 mg; Sod 145 mg.
    Nutritional information includes entire amount of marinade.

VIDALIA ONION CASSEROLE

8 Vidalia onions
1/2 cup margarine
1/2 cup Parmesan cheese

1 cup butter cracker
crumbs

Cut onions into thin slices. Sauté in margarine in skillet until tender. Layer onions, cheese and cracker crumbs 1/2 at a time in baking dish. Bake at 325 degrees for 30 minutes. Yield: 8 servings.

Approx Per Serving: Cal 231; Prot 5 g; Carbo 20 g; Fiber 3 g; T Fat 17 g; Chol 4 mg; Sod 336 mg.

PEA PODS AND ALMONDS

1/2 cup water
1 tablespoon soy sauce
1 1/2 teaspoons cornstarch
1 teaspoon instant
chicken bouillon
2 tablespoons slivered
almonds

2 tablespoons margarine
1 10-ounce package
frozen pea pods, thawed
1 4-ounce can sliced
mushrooms

Combine water, soy sauce, cornstarch and bouillon in small bowl; mix well. Stir-fry almonds in margarine in skillet for 2 minutes. Add pea pods. Stir-fry for 2 minutes. Stir in mushrooms and cornstarch mixture. Cook for 1 to 2 minutes or until thickened, stirring constantly. Yield: 4 servings.

Approx Per Serving: Cal 128; Prot 4 g; Carbo 10 g; Fiber 3 g; T Fat 8 g; Chol 0 mg; Sod 737 mg.

OVEN-FRIED POTATOES

3 medium potatoes
3 tablespoons melted
  margarine
1¹/₂ teaspoons marjoram

¹/₂ teaspoon paprika
¹/₂ teaspoon garlic powder
Salt and pepper to taste
¹/₄ cup Parmesan cheese

Cut unpeeled potatoes into thin slices. Combine margarine, marjoram, paprika, garlic powder, salt and pepper in bowl. Coat potato slices with margarine mixture. Arrange in single layer on baking sheet. Bake at 350 degrees for 20 minutes or until potatoes begin to brown; turn with spatula. Sprinkle with cheese. Bake for 10 minutes longer. Yield: 4 servings.

Approx Per Serving: Cal 264; Prot 6 g; Carbo 39 g; Fiber 4 g;
    T Fat 10 g; Chol 4 mg; Sod 207 mg.

SWISS CHEESE POTATOES

1 2-pound package
   frozen hashed brown
   potatoes
2 cups whipping cream

2 cups shredded Swiss
  cheese
¹/₂ cup melted butter
Salt and pepper to taste

Thaw frozen potatoes slightly. Combine with whipping cream, cheese, butter, salt and pepper in bowl; mix well. Spoon into large baking dish. Bake at 350 degrees for 1 hour and 15 minutes or until brown and bubbly. Yield: 12 servings.

Approx Per Serving: Cal 441; Prot 9 g; Carbo 23 g; Fiber 2 g;
    T Fat 36 g; Chol 92 mg; Sod 154 mg.

SQUASH CASSEROLE

2 pounds yellow squash,
  chopped
1 medium onion, chopped
3 tablespoons melted
  margarine

2 eggs, beaten
Sage, paprika, salt and
  pepper to taste
2 cups shredded
  Cheddar cheese

Cook squash in a small amount of water in saucepan until tender; drain. Combine with onion, margarine, eggs, sage, paprika, salt and pepper in bowl; mix well. Stir in half the cheese. Spoon into buttered baking dish. Sprinkle with remaining cheese and additional paprika. Bake at 350 degrees for 30 minutes or until set. Yield: 6 servings.

Approx Per Serving: Cal 268; Prot 14 g; Carbo 9 g; Fiber 3 g;
    T Fat 20 g; Chol 111 mg; Sod 328 mg.

SPINACH CASSEROLE

2 10-ounce packages
  frozen chopped spinach
8 ounces cream cheese,
  softened

1 small onion, chopped
1/2 cup milk
1/2 cup shredded Cheddar
  cheese

Cook spinach using package directions; place in colander. Press with spoon to drain well. Combine cream cheese and onion in bowl; mix well. Add milk gradually, mixing until smooth. Mix in spinach. Spoon into greased 1-quart baking dish. Sprinkle with cheese. Bake at 350 degrees for 20 minutes. Yield: 8 servings.

Approx Per Serving: Cal 162; Prot 7 g; Carbo 6 g; Fiber 2 g;
    T Fat 13 g; Chol 40 mg; Sod 195 mg.

SWEET POTATO CASSEROLE

3 cups mashed cooked
  sweet potatoes
2 eggs, beaten
1/2 cup milk
1/2 cup margarine,
  softened

1 teaspoon vanilla extract
1 cup packed brown
  sugar
1/2 cup flour
1/3 cup margarine
1 cup chopped pecans

Combine sweet potatoes, eggs, milk, 1/2 cup margarine and vanilla in bowl; mix well. Spoon into baking dish. Mix brown sugar and flour in bowl. Add 1/3 cup margarine and pecans; mix until crumbly. Sprinkle over casserole. Bake at 350 degrees for 25 minutes. Yield: 8 servings.

Approx Per Serving: Cal 527; Prot 6 g; Carbo 59 g; Fiber 3 g;
    T Fat 31 g; Chol 55 mg; Sod 329 mg.

BAKED STUFFED TOMATOES

4 large tomatoes
2 cups bread crumbs
6 tablespoons Parmesan
  cheese

1/2 cup melted margarine
3 tablespoons Italian
  salad dressing

Cut tomatoes into halves; place in shallow baking dish. Combine bread crumbs, cheese, margarine and salad dressing in bowl; mix well. Spoon over tomatoes. Bake at 350 degrees for 15 to 20 minutes or until tomatoes are heated through and crumbs are lightly browned. May broil for 4 minutes if preferred. Yield: 8 servings.

Approx Per Serving: Cal 254; Prot 6 g; Carbo 22 g; Fiber 2 g;
    T Fat 17 g; Chol 4 mg; Sod 420 mg.

ZUCCHINI BAKE

2 cups thinly sliced
  zucchini
1 large tomato, thinly
  sliced
1 large onion, thinly
  sliced

1 teaspoon thyme
2 tablespoons Parmesan
  cheese
1 tablespoon margarine

Layer zucchini, tomato, onion, thyme and cheese 1/2 at a time in greased 1 1/2-quart glass dish. Dot with margarine. Bake at 350 degrees for 30 minutes or until vegetables are tender-crisp. Yield: 4 servings.

Approx Per Serving: Cal 66; Prot 3 g; Carbo 6 g; Fiber 2 g;
    T Fat 4 g; Chol 2 mg; Sod 85 mg.

ZUCCHINI SAUTÉ

2 cups sliced zucchini
1 cup sliced onion
3 tablespoons margarine

1 cup chopped tomatoes
1/4 cup Romano cheese

Sauté zucchini and onion in margarine in skillet for 10 minutes or until vegetables are tender. Add tomatoes. Cook over low heat for 5 minutes. Sprinkle with cheese. Yield: 6 servings.

Approx Per Serving: Cal 87; Prot 2 g; Carbo 5 g; Fiber 1 g;
    T Fat 7 g; Chol 4 mg; Sod 118 mg.

SLOW-COOKER BAKED APPLES

8 apples
1/3 cup raisins
1/3 cup chopped pecans
1/3 cup packed brown
 sugar

1 teaspoon cinnamon
1/2 teaspoon nutmeg
2 tablespoons margarine
1/2 cup apple cider
1 tablespoon lemon juice

Peel top 1/3 of apples; remove and discard cores. Fill cavities with mixture of raisins, pecans and brown sugar. Place in slow-cooker. Sprinkle with cinnamon and nutmeg; dot with margarine. Add cider and lemon juice. Cook on Low for 8 hours to overnight. Yield: 8 servings.

Approx Per Serving: Cal 169; Prot 1 g; Carbo 37 g; Fiber 4 g;
 T Fat 3 g; Chol 0 mg; Sod 40 mg.

BAKED PINEAPPLE

1 20-ounce can
 unsweetened pineapple
 chunks
3 tablespoons sugar
6 tablespoons melted
 butter

3 tablespoons flour
5 ounces Cheddar
 cheese, shredded
1 cup butter cracker
 crumbs

Drain pineapple, reserving 3 tablespoons juice. Combine pineapple, reserved juice, sugar, butter, flour and cheese in bowl; mix well. Spoon into baking dish; top with cracker crumbs. Bake at 350 degrees for 30 minutes or until bubbly. Yield: 6 servings.

Approx Per Serving: Cal 362; Prot 8 g; Carbo 34 g; Fiber 1 g;
 T Fat 24 g; Chol 56 mg; Sod 385 mg.

GARLIC CHEESE GRITS

1 cup quick-cooking grits
1/2 teaspoon salt
3 cups water
1/2 cup margarine

1 6-ounce roll garlic
   cheese
2 eggs
1 1/2 cups (about) milk

Cook grits with salt in water in saucepan until thickened. Melt margarine with cheese in saucepan over low heat. Add grits; mix well. Beat eggs in measuring cup. Add enough milk to measure 2 cups. Add to grits; mix well. Spoon into greased 1 1/2-quart baking dish. Bake at 350 degrees for 45 minutes or until set. Yield: 8 servings.

Approx Per Serving: Cal 246; Prot 8 g; Carbo 6 g; Fiber 1 g;
     T Fat 21 g; Chol 80 mg; Sod 678 mg.

GREEN RICE

2 tablespoons finely
   chopped onion
1/4 teaspoon minced garlic
2 tablespoons butter
1/2 cup shredded Cheddar
   cheese

2 cups cooked rice
1/2 cup finely chopped
   parsley
2 eggs
1 1/4 cups milk
1 teaspoon salt

Sauté onion and garlic in butter in skillet over low heat for 4 minutes. Add cheese, rice and parsley; mix well. Spoon into greased baking dish. Blend eggs, milk and salt in small bowl. Pour over rice. Place baking dish in pan of water in oven. Bake at 350 degrees for 40 minutes. Yield: 6 servings.

Approx Per Serving: Cal 207; Prot 8 g; Carbo 20 g; Fiber 1 g;
     T Fat 11 g; Chol 98 mg; Sod 492 mg.

Choose paper items made from recycled paper, such as bathroom tissue, paper towels, cereal boxes, napkins, writing paper, greeting cards and envelopes.

Effortless

Breads

MAYONNAISE BISCUITS

2 cups self-rising flour
1 tablespoon baking
powder

³/4 cup mayonnaise
³/4 to 1 cup milk

Mix flour and baking powder in bowl. Add mayonnaise and enough milk to make batter slightly thicker than cake batter; mix well. Spoon into greased muffin cups. Bake at 425 degrees for 15 minutes or until golden brown. Yield: 12 servings.

Approx Per Serving: Cal 186; Prot 3 g; Carbo 17 g; Fiber 1 g;
      T Fat 12 g; Chol 11 mg; Sod 394 mg.

PARMESAN BISCUITS

2 10-count cans biscuits
¹/2 cup melted butter

1 cup Parmesan cheese
Dillweed to taste

Dip each biscuit into butter; roll in Parmesan cheese to coat. Arrange biscuits in 9x13-inch baking pan. Sprinkle with dillweed. Bake at 450 degrees until golden brown and crusty. Yield: 20 servings.

Approx Per Serving: Cal 124; Prot 3 g; Carbo 10 g; Fiber <1 g;
      T Fat 8 g; Chol 17 mg; Sod 363 mg.

SAVORY BLEU CHEESE BISCUITS

2 10-count cans biscuits
²/3 cup melted butter

¹/2 cup crumbled bleu
cheese

Arrange biscuits in greased 9x13-inch baking pan. Combine butter and cheese in bowl; mix well. Spoon over biscuits. Bake at 400 degrees for 15 minutes or until golden brown. Yield: 20 servings.

Approx Per Serving: Cal 129; Prot 2 g; Carbo 10 g; Fiber <1 g;
      T Fat 9 g; Chol 20 mg; Sod 340 mg.

SAUSAGE AND SOUR CREAM BRUNCH BISCUITS

1 8-ounce package brown and serve sausage links	1 cup melted margarine 1 cup sour cream 2 cups self-rising flour

Cook sausages using package directions for about half the time; drain on paper towels. Cut sausages into 1/4-inch slices. Blend margarine and sour cream in bowl. Add flour; mix well. Spoon into ungreased miniature muffin cups. Press sausage slices lightly over tops. Bake at 450 degrees for 15 minutes or until golden brown. Yield: 30 servings.

Approx Per Serving: Cal 129; Prot 2 g; Carbo 7 g; Fiber <1 g;
   T Fat 11 g; Chol 9 mg; Sod 226 mg.

QUICK COFFEE CAKE

1/2 cup margarine 2 cups baking mix 1 cup sugar 1 cup milk 1/2 cup chopped pecans	1 1/2 cups packed brown sugar 1/2 cup coconut 1 tablespoon cinnamon

Melt margarine in 9x13-inch baking pan. Combine baking mix, sugar and milk in bowl; mix well. Pour over margarine in baking pan; do not stir. Combine pecans, brown sugar, coconut and cinnamon in small bowl; mix well. Sprinkle over batter. Bake at 350 degrees for 30 minutes. Yield: 12 servings.

Approx Per Serving: Cal 361; Prot 2 g; Carbo 57 g; Fiber 1 g;
   T Fat 15 g; Chol 3 mg; Sod 301 mg.

 Think "precycle." Shop for items with the minimum amount of packaging.

OVERNIGHT COMPANY COFFEE CAKE

12 1-ounce frozen yeast
   rolls
1½ cups packed brown
   sugar
1 cup chopped pecans

2 teaspoons cinnamon
1 6-ounce package
   vanilla instant pudding
   mix
1 cup butter, softened

Arrange frozen rolls in greased bundt pan. Combine brown sugar, pecans, cinnamon and dry pudding mix in bowl; mix well. Sprinkle over rolls. Dot with butter. Place bundt pan in cold oven. Let rise, loosely covered, overnight. Remove pan; preheat oven to 350 degrees. Bake coffee cake for 20 to 30 minutes or until golden brown. Invert onto serving plate. Yield: 12 servings.

Approx Per Serving: Cal 443; Prot 3 g; Carbo 56 g; Fiber 2 g;
   T Fat 24 g; Chol 41 mg; Sod 391 mg.

PECAN MONKEY BREAD

3 10-count cans
   buttermilk biscuits
⅔ cup sugar
1 tablespoon cinnamon

½ cup melted butter
1 cup packed brown
   sugar
1 cup chopped pecans

Cut biscuits into fourths. Roll in mixture of sugar and cinnamon. Layer in greased bundt pan. Combine butter and brown sugar in bowl. Stir until well blended. Drizzle over biscuits. Sprinkle with pecans. Bake at 350 degrees for 35 minutes or until brown. Invert onto serving plate.
Yield: 15 servings.

Approx Per Serving: Cal 327; Prot 4 g; Carbo 44 g; Fiber 1 g;
   T Fat 16 g; Chol 19 mg; Sod 556 mg.

BEST CORN BREAD

2 cups baking mix
3/4 cup sugar
3/4 cup yellow cornmeal
1/2 teaspoon baking
  powder

2 eggs, beaten
1 cup milk
3/4 cup melted butter
1 teaspoon vanilla extract

Combine baking mix, sugar, cornmeal and baking powder in bowl. Add eggs, milk, butter and vanilla; mix well. Pour into greased 8x8-inch baking pan. Bake at 350 degrees for 35 to 40 minutes or until golden brown. Serve hot with butter and honey. Yield: 9 servings.

Approx Per Serving: Cal 399; Prot 5 g; Carbo 46 g; Fiber 1 g;
    T Fat 22 g; Chol 92 mg; Sod 527 mg.

BROCCOLI CORN BREAD

1 10-ounce package
  frozen chopped broccoli
1 cup chopped onion
1 cup cottage cheese

1/2 cup melted butter
4 eggs, beaten
1 7-ounce package corn
  muffin mix

Combine broccoli and onion in glass bowl. Microwave, covered, on High for 2 to 3 minutes or until broccoli thaws. Add cottage cheese, butter and eggs; mix well. Add muffin mix; stir just until moistened. Pour into greased 9x9-inch baking pan. Bake at 400 degrees for 35 minutes or until golden brown. Yield: 9 servings.

Approx Per Serving: Cal 207; Prot 7 g; Carbo 12 g; Fiber 1 g;
    T Fat 15 g; Chol 126 mg; Sod 317 mg.

MEXICAN CORN BREAD

1 6-ounce package corn
  bread mix
1 12-ounce can
  Mexicorn, drained
1/2 cup chopped onion

1 4-ounce can chopped
  green chilies
3 cups shredded
  Cheddar cheese

Prepare corn bread mix using package directions. Add corn, onion, green chilies and 2 cups cheese; mix well. Pour into preheated greased cast-iron skillet. Sprinkle remaining cheese over top. Bake at 375 degrees for 40 minutes or until golden brown. Yield: 8 servings.

Approx Per Serving: Cal 429; Prot 16 g; Carbo 43 g; Fiber 3 g;
  T Fat 24 g; Chol 108 mg; Sod 800 mg.

CORN LIGHT BREAD

2 cups cornmeal
1 cup sugar
1/2 cup flour

1 teaspoon salt
1 teaspoon soda
2 cups buttermilk

Combine cornmeal, sugar, flour and salt in bowl. Dissolve soda in buttermilk. Add to cornmeal mixture; mix well. Pour into buttered 5x9-inch loaf pan. Bake for 1 1/4 hours or until golden brown and firm in center. Yield: 14 servings.

Approx Per Serving: Cal 157; Prot 3 g; Carbo 35 g; Fiber 2 g;
  T Fat 1 g; Chol 1 mg; Sod 248 mg.

 Spark ignition instead of a pilot light can cut a stove's gas use by 40 to 50 percent.

COLONIAL BROWN QUICK BREAD

4 cups whole wheat flour
1¹/₃ cups all-purpose flour
2 cups packed brown sugar

1 teaspoon salt
4 teaspoons soda
4 cups buttermilk

Combine flours, brown sugar, salt and soda in large bowl. Add buttermilk gradually, mixing well after each addition. Pour into 2 greased 5x9-inch loaf pans. Bake at 350 degrees for 1 hour or until loaves test done. Invert onto wire rack. Slice and serve warm. Yield: 24 servings.

Approx Per Serving: Cal 177; Prot 5 g; Carbo 39 g; Fiber 3 g;
T Fat 1 g; Chol 2 mg; Sod 277 mg.

QUICK CHEESE LOAF

2 cups baking mix
³/₄ cup milk
2 eggs, beaten

2 teaspoons dry mustard
1¹/₂ cups shredded sharp Cheddar cheese

Combine baking mix, milk, eggs and dry mustard in bowl; mix well. Stir in cheese. Spoon into greased 5x9-inch loaf pan. Bake at 350 degrees for 40 to 50 minutes or until golden brown. Invert onto wire rack. Slice and serve warm. Yield: 12 servings.

Approx Per Serving: Cal 170; Prot 7 g; Carbo 15 g; Fiber 0 g;
T Fat 9 g; Chol 52 mg; Sod 370 mg.

 Keep the refrigerator between 38 and 42 degrees. If it is kept only 10 degrees colder than this, energy consumption will go up 25 percent.

CHEESY BRUNCH BREAD

3/4 cup milk
1/2 cup Italian salad
  dressing
1   5-ounce jar Old
  English cheese
2 eggs, beaten
2 3/4 cups flour
1 1/2 teaspoons baking
  powder

1/4 teaspoon soda
2 tablespoons sugar
1 teaspoon salt
1 teaspoon dry mustard
3/4 cup finely chopped
  pepperoni
1/4 cup chopped green
  bell pepper

Combine milk, salad dressing, cheese and eggs in bowl; mix well. Combine flour, baking powder, soda, sugar, salt and dry mustard in bowl; mix well. Add to cheese mixture; stir just until moistened. Fold in pepperoni and green pepper. Spoon into greased 5x9-inch loaf pan. Bake at 350 degrees for 50 minutes or until golden brown. Invert onto wire rack. Slice and serve warm. Store any leftover bread in refrigerator. Yield: 12 servings.

Approx Per Serving: Cal 291; Prot 10 g; Carbo 27 g; Fiber 1 g;
  T Fat 17 g; Chol 50 mg; Sod 732 mg.

CRANBERRY AND ORANGE BREAD

1   8-ounce package
  orange muffin mix
1 cup chopped pecans

1   8-ounce can whole
  cranberry sauce

Prepare muffin mix using package directions. Add pecans and cranberry sauce; mix well. Pour into greased 5x9-inch loaf pan. Bake at 350 degrees for 30 minutes or until bread tests done. Invert onto wire rack. Slice and serve warm. Yield: 12 servings.

Approx Per Serving: Cal 196; Prot 3 g; Carbo 25 g; Fiber 3 g;
  T Fat 10 g; Chol 30 mg; Sod 153 mg.

EASY HERBED LOAF

1 16-inch loaf French
 bread
1/2 cup melted butter
1/4 cup minced green
 onions

1/4 cup minced parsley
1/8 teaspoon thyme
1/8 teaspoon marjoram
Garlic salt to taste

Slice loaf into 1-inch thick slices, cutting to but not through bottom. Combine butter, green onions, parsley, thyme, marjoram and garlic salt in small bowl; mix well. Spread on bread slices. Wrap in foil. Bake at 400 degrees for 15 minutes. Yield: 16 servings.

Approx Per Serving: Cal 133; Prot 3 g; Carbo 15 g; Fiber 1 g;
 T Fat 7 g; Chol 16 mg; Sod 213 mg.

ONION CRESCENT STICKS

2 3-ounce cans
 French-fried onions
2 tablespoons melted
 margarine
2 eggs, beaten

1/2 teaspoon parsley
 flakes
1/4 teaspoon garlic powder
1 8-count can crescent
 rolls

Crush French-fried onions in shallow dish. Combine margarine, eggs, parsley flakes and garlic powder in shallow dish; mix well. Separate roll dough into 4 rectangles; press perforations to seal. Cut each rectangle into 8 strips. Dip strips into egg mixture; coat with crushed onions. Place on ungreased baking sheet. Bake at 375 degrees for 12 minutes or until brown. Yield: 32 servings.

Approx Per Serving: Cal 54; Prot 1 g; Carbo 5 g; Fiber <1 g;
 T Fat 3 g; Chol 15 mg; Sod 79 mg.

MIX-IN-THE-PAN PUMPKIN BREAD

1 cup canned pumpkin
$^1/_3$ cup oil
3 eggs, beaten
1$^1/_4$ cups sugar

2$^1/_3$ cups baking mix
2 teaspoons cinnamon
$^1/_2$ cup raisins

Combine pumpkin, oil, eggs, sugar, baking mix and cinnamon in greased 5x9-inch loaf pan. Mix for 1 minute. Stir in raisins. Bake at 350 degrees for 45 minutes or until loaf tests done. Cool in pan for 10 minutes. Remove to wire rack to cool completely. Yield: 12 servings.

Approx Per Serving: Cal 287; Prot 4 g; Carbo 45 g; Fiber 1 g;
   T Fat 11 g; Chol 53 mg; Sod 328 mg.

APPLESAUCE MUFFINS

1 cup margarine, softened
2 cups sugar
2 eggs
1 teaspoon vanilla extract
4 cups flour
2 teaspoons soda
2 teaspoons allspice

1 tablespoon cinnamon
1 teaspoon cloves
1   16-ounce can
   unsweetened
   applesauce
1 cup raisins
1 cup chopped pecans

Cream margarine and sugar in mixer bowl until light and fluffy. Add eggs and vanilla; mix well. Sift in mixture of flour, soda, allspice, cinnamon and cloves alternately with applesauce, mixing just until blended after each addition. Stir in raisins and pecans. Spoon into greased muffin cups. Bake at 375 degrees for 20 minutes or until golden brown. Yield: 24 servings.

Approx Per Serving: Cal 282; Prot 4 g; Carbo 43 g; Fiber 2 g;
   T Fat 11 g; Chol 18 mg; Sod 166 mg.

BANANA-PECAN MUFFINS

2 cups mashed bananas
1 cup sugar
2 eggs, beaten
3/4 cup melted margarine

2 cups flour
2 teaspoons soda
3 tablespoons buttermilk
1 cup chopped pecans

Combine bananas, sugar and eggs in bowl; mix well. Blend in margarine gradually. Add flour, soda and buttermilk; mix well. Stir in pecans. Spoon into greased muffin cups. Bake at 300 degrees for 40 minutes or until muffins test done. Yield: 12 servings.

Approx Per Serving: Cal 357; Prot 5 g; Carbo 43 g; Fiber 2 g;
    T Fat 19 g; Chol 36 mg; Sod 287 mg.

CHEDDAR-PIMENTO MUFFINS

2 cups flour
3 1/2 teaspoons baking
  powder
1/2 teaspoon salt
1 teaspoon paprika
1 cup shredded Cheddar
  cheese

1 4-ounce jar chopped
  pimento, drained
1 egg, beaten
1 cup milk
1/4 cup melted margarine
Tabasco sauce to taste

Combine flour, baking powder, salt, paprika, cheese and pimento in bowl; mix well. Make well in center. Beat egg with milk, margarine and Tabasco sauce in bowl. Pour into well in cheese mixture; mix just until moistened. Fill greased muffin cups 2/3 full. Bake at 425 degrees for 20 minutes or until brown. Yield: 12 servings.

Approx Per Serving: Cal 171; Prot 6 g; Carbo 18 g; Fiber 1 g;
    T Fat 8 g; Chol 30 mg; Sod 303 mg.

MINIATURE PECAN MUFFINS

2 cups baking mix
1/2 cup sugar
1/4 cup flour

1 egg, beaten
3/4 cup milk
1 cup chopped pecans

Combine baking mix, sugar and flour in bowl. Beat egg with milk. Add to flour mixture; mix well. Stir in pecans. Fill greased and floured miniature muffin cups 2/3 full. Bake at 350 degrees until brown. Serve hot. May remove to wire rack to cool, scoop out centers, stuff with chicken salad or other favorite filling and serve as appetizers. Yield: 18 servings.

Approx Per Serving: Cal 143; Prot 2 g; Carbo 18 g; Fiber <1 g; T Fat 7 g; Chol 13 mg; Sod 185 mg.

ITALIAN-STYLE POPOVERS

2 eggs
1/2 cup milk
1/2 cup water
1 cup flour

1 tablespoon Italian salad
   dressing mix
1/4 teaspoon salt
1 tablespoon oil

Combine eggs, milk, water, flour, salad dressing mix and salt in small mixer bowl. Beat at medium speed for 1 1/2 minutes. Add oil. Beat for 30 seconds longer. Pour into greased 6-ounce custard cups. Bake at 350 degrees for 25 minutes or until golden brown. Yield: 6 servings.

Approx Per Serving: Cal 137; Prot 5 g; Carbo 18 g; Fiber 1 g; T Fat 5 g; Chol 74 mg; Sod 254 mg.

OVEN FRENCH TOAST

1/2 cup margarine
1 cup packed brown
sugar
1 teaspoon cinnamon

12 slices raisin bread
4 eggs, beaten
1 1/2 cups milk

Melt margarine in 9x13-inch baking pan in hot oven. Add brown sugar and cinnamon; mix well. Arrange bread slices in double layer in prepared baking pan. Beat eggs with milk. Pour over bread slices. Chill, tightly covered, in refrigerator overnight. Bake, uncovered, at 350 degrees for 45 minutes. Serve with warm syrup and sprinkle of confectioners' sugar. Yield: 12 servings.

Approx Per Serving: Cal 250; Prot 5 g; Carbo 33 g; Fiber 1 g;
T Fat 12 g; Chol 75 mg; Sod 225 mg.

SIXTY-MINUTE ROLLS

2 envelopes dry yeast
1/4 cup lukewarm water
1 1/4 cups milk
3 tablespoons sugar

1/4 teaspoon salt
1/4 cup margarine
3 cups flour

Dissolve yeast in warm water. Heat milk, sugar, salt and margarine in saucepan just until margarine melts; remove from heat. Add to flour in bowl. Add yeast; mix well. Let stand, covered, in warm place for 15 minutes. Dough will be very soft; do not knead. Shape into small balls with greased hands. Arrange 3 balls in each of 24 greased muffin cups. Let rise, covered, in warm place for 15 minutes. Bake at 450 degrees for 10 minutes or until golden brown. Yield: 24 servings.

Approx Per Serving: Cal 89; Prot 2 g; Carbo 14 g; Fiber 1 g;
T Fat 2 g; Chol 2 mg; Sod 51 mg.

SOUR CREAM YEAST ROLLS

1 envelope dry yeast
1/4 cup warm water
2 cups sour cream

2 tablespoons sugar
1/4 teaspoon soda
51/4 cups baking mix

Dissolve yeast in warm water. Blend sour cream, sugar and soda in large bowl. Add yeast and 2 cups baking mix; mix well. Mix in 3 cups baking mix; dough will be soft. Knead on surface sprinkled with remaining 1/4 cup baking mix until smooth and elastic. Shape into walnut-sized balls; arrange in greased 9x13-inch baking pan. Let rise, covered, until doubled in bulk. Bake at 375 degrees for 15 minutes or until golden brown. Yield: 48 servings.

Approx Per Serving: Cal 83; Prot 2 g; Carbo 11 g; Fiber 1 g;
T Fat 5 g; Chol 5 mg; Sod 183 mg.

CRUSTY ROLLS

1 loaf frozen bread
  dough, thawed
1/2 cup seasoned bread
  crumbs

1 teaspoon poppy seed
2 tablespoons melted
  margarine

Divide dough into 12 portions; shape into rolls. Mix bread crumbs and poppy seed in bowl. Dip rolls in margarine; roll in crumb mixture. Place 3 inches apart on greased baking sheet. Let rise, covered, for 11/2 hours or until doubled in bulk. Bake at 375 degrees for 15 to 20 minutes or until brown. Yield: 12 servings.

Approx Per Serving: Cal 133; Prot 4 g; Carbo 21 g; Fiber 1 g;
T Fat 4 g; Chol <1 mg; Sod 245 mg.

Clock-Watching

Desserts

APPLE CRISP

6 apples, peeled, sliced
1/2 cup flour
3/4 cup packed brown
   sugar
1/2 teaspoon cinnamon

1/2 teaspoon nutmeg
1/2 cup quick-cooking oats
1/2 cup chopped pecans
3/4 cup melted margarine

Spread apples in baking dish. Combine flour, brown sugar, cinnamon, nutmeg, oats and pecans in bowl; mix well. Add margarine; mix well. Sprinkle evenly over apples. Bake at 375 degrees for 35 minutes. Serve with ice cream or whipped topping. Yield: 8 servings.

Approx Per Serving: Cal 381; Prot 3 g; Carbo 45 g; Fiber 3 g;
   T Fat 23 g; Chol 0 mg; Sod 210 mg.

BANANA PUDDING

1 6-ounce package
   vanilla instant
   pudding mix
3 cups milk
1 14-ounce can
   sweetened condensed
   milk

8 ounces whipped
   topping
1 12-ounce package
   vanilla wafers
6 bananas, sliced

Prepare pudding mix with milk, using package directions. Add condensed milk; mix well. Fold in whipped topping. Layer vanilla wafers, bananas and pudding 1/2 at a time in large dish. Chill until serving time. Yield: 12 servings.

Approx Per Serving: Cal 440; Prot 7 g; Carbo 72 g; Fiber 1 g;
   T Fat 15 g; Chol 37 mg; Sod 274 mg.

BLACKBERRY COBBLER

4 cups blackberries
1 cup sugar
1/2 cup margarine
1 cup flour

1 cup sugar
1 cup milk
2 teaspoons baking
powder

Combine blackberries and 1 cup sugar in bowl. Let stand for several minutes. Melt margarine in 9x13-inch baking dish. Combine flour, 1 cup sugar, milk and baking powder in bowl; mix well. Spoon into prepared dish. Spoon blackberries and juice over batter; do not stir. Bake at 350 degrees for 45 minutes or until golden brown. Yield: 10 servings.

Approx Per Serving: Cal 327; Prot 3 g; Carbo 58 g; Fiber 4 g;
T Fat 10 g; Chol 3 mg; Sod 184 mg.

BREAD PUDDING

1 1/2 cups bread cubes
1 tablespoon flour
3 eggs, beaten
1 cup sugar

2 cups milk
1 teaspoon vanilla extract
1 tablespoon melted
margarine

Place bread cubes in 8x8-inch baking dish sprayed with nonstick cooking spray. Sprinkle flour over bread. Combine eggs, sugar, milk, vanilla and margarine in bowl. Pour over bread. Bake at 350 degrees for 30 to 40 minutes or until golden brown. Serve with hard sauce or ice cream. Yield: 6 servings.

Approx Per Serving: Cal 339; Prot 9 g; Carbo 57 g; Fiber 1 g;
T Fat 9 g; Chol 119 mg; Sod 276 mg.

CHERRY DELIGHT

1 cup sour cream
2 cups milk
1 6-ounce package
  vanilla instant
  pudding mix

30 graham cracker
  squares
1 21-ounce can cherry
  pie filling

Combine sour cream and milk in bowl. Beat with rotary beater until smooth. Add pudding mix. Beat for 2 minutes or until thickened and smooth. Layer graham crackers and pudding 1/2 at a time in dish. Top with pie filling. Chill, covered, for 3 hours or longer. Cut into squares. May substitute yogurt for sour cream. Yield: 12 servings.

Approx Per Serving: Cal 241; Prot 3 g; Carbo 42 g; Fiber 1 g;
    T Fat 7 g; Chol 14 mg; Sod 244 mg.

FAVORITE CHOCOLATE TREAT

1 angel food cake
1 6-ounce package
  chocolate instant
  pudding mix

4 cups whipped topping
1 1 1/2-ounce milk
  chocolate candy bar,
  shaved

Tear cake into bite-sized pieces. Place in 9x13-inch dish. Prepare pudding mix using package directions. Spoon over cake. Spread whipped topping over pudding. Top with shaved chocolate. Chill until serving time. Yield: 12 servings.

Approx Per Serving: Cal 326; Prot 6 g; Carbo 54 g; Fiber <1 g;
    T Fat 10 g; Chol 10 mg; Sod 572 mg.

NO-BAKE PINEAPPLE DESSERT

1/2 cup melted butter
1 cup sugar
1 egg
1 8-ounce can crushed
   pineapple

12 ounces whipped
   topping
1 12-ounce package
   vanilla wafers

Combine butter and sugar in mixer bowl; mix well. Beat in egg. Fold in undrained pineapple and whipped topping. Arrange 1 layer vanilla wafers in 9x13-inch dish. Spread pineapple mixture in prepared dish. Crush remaining vanilla wafers. Sprinkle over top. Chill overnight. Yield: 12 servings.

Approx Per Serving: Cal 375; Prot 2 g; Carbo 48 g; Fiber 0 g;
    T Fat 20 g; Chol 56 mg; Sod 184 mg.

DESSERT PIZZA

1 16-ounce roll sugar
   cookie dough
8 ounces cream cheese,
   softened
1 teaspoon vanilla extract

1/2 cup sugar
1 21-ounce can
   strawberry pie filling
1 cup crushed pineapple
2 bananas, sliced

Slice cookie dough 1/4 inch thick. Arrange slices close together in pizza pan. Bake at 350 degrees for 10 to 12 minutes or until light brown. Cool completely. Beat cream cheese, vanilla and sugar in mixer bowl until smooth. Spread over cookie layer. Layer pie filling, pineapple and bananas over creamed layer. Chill until serving time. Yield: 12 servings.

Approx Per Serving: Cal 354; Prot 3 g; Carbo 52 g; Fiber 1 g;
    T Fat 16 g; Chol 44 mg; Sod 277 mg.

FROSTY PUDDING CONES

²/₃ cup sweetened
  condensed milk
2 tablespoons lemon juice
1 cup peach yogurt

6 sugar ice cream cones
6 tablespoons whipped
  topping

Combine sweetened condensed milk and lemon juice in bowl; mix well. Stir in yogurt. Spoon into sugar cones, leaving ¹/₂ inch space at top. Place in upright glasses or tall jars. Freeze for 3 hours or until firm. Top with whipped topping. Yield: 6 servings.

Approx Per Serving: Cal 203; Prot 5 g; Carbo 36 g; Fiber <1 g;
  T Fat 5 g; Chol 13 mg; Sod 100 mg.

PUMPKIN DESSERT

1 2-layer package
  yellow cake mix
¹/₂ cup melted margarine
1 egg
1 16-ounce can
  pumpkin pie filling
2 cups milk

2 eggs
¹/₄ cup margarine,
  softened
¹/₂ cup chopped pecans
¹/₄ cup sugar
1 teaspoon cinnamon

Reserve 1 cup cake mix. Combine remaining cake mix, ¹/₂ cup melted margarine and 1 egg in bowl; mix well. Press into 9x13-inch baking dish. Combine pumpkin, milk and 2 eggs in bowl; mix well. Pour over crumb layer. Mix ¹/₄ cup margarine, reserved 1 cup cake mix, pecans, sugar and cinnamon in bowl until crumbly. Sprinkle over pumpkin mixture. Bake at 325 degrees for 1 hour or until set. Serve warm with whipped topping. Yield: 12 servings.

Approx Per Serving: Cal 391; Prot 6 g; Carbo 46 g; Fiber 1 g;
  T Fat 21 g; Chol 59 mg; Sod 432 mg.

STRAWBERRY SQUARES

1 cup sifted flour
1/4 cup packed brown
  sugar
1/2 cup chopped walnuts
1/2 cup melted butter
2 egg whites

1 cup sugar
2 cups sliced
  strawberries
2 tablespoons lemon juice
1 cup whipping cream,
  whipped

Combine flour, brown sugar, walnuts and melted butter in bowl; mix well. Spread in shallow baking pan. Bake at 350 degrees for 20 minutes, stirring occasionally. Crumble mixture. Sprinkle 2/3 of the crumbs into 9x13-inch dish. Combine egg whites, sugar, strawberries and lemon juice in mixer bowl. Beat at high speed for 15 minutes or until very light and stiff. Fold in whipped cream. Spread in prepared pan. Sprinkle with remaining crumbs. Freeze for 6 hours or longer. Yield: 12 servings.

Approx Per Serving: Cal 295; Prot 3 g; Carbo 32 g; Fiber 1 g;
  T Fat 18 g; Chol 48 mg; Sod 84 mg.

APPLE SWIRL CAKE

1/4 cup sugar
2 teaspoons cinnamon
1 2/3 cups applesauce

1 2-layer package
  yellow cake mix
3 eggs

Mix sugar and cinnamon in small bowl. Sprinkle 1 tablespoon of the mixture into greased 10-inch bundt pan. Combine applesauce, cake mix and eggs in mixer bowl. Mix using cake mix package directions. Pour half the batter into prepared pan. Sprinkle with remaining cinnamon-sugar. Top with remaining batter. Bake at 350 degrees for 35 to 45 minutes or until cake tests done. Cool in pan for 15 minutes. Invert onto serving plate. Yield: 16 servings.

Approx Per Serving: Cal 184; Prot 3 g; Carbo 35 g; Fiber <1 g;
  T Fat 4 g; Chol 40 mg; Sod 210 mg.

APRICOT NECTAR CAKE

1 2-layer package lemon
  supreme cake mix
1/2 cup sugar
4 eggs
1/2 cup oil

1 cup apricot nectar
2 cups confectioners'
  sugar
1/4 cup lemon juice

Combine cake mix, sugar, eggs, oil and apricot nectar in mixer bowl. Beat at low speed until blended. Beat at high speed for 6 minutes. Pour into greased and floured tube pan. Bake at 350 degrees for 50 minutes or until cake tests done. Cool in pan for 5 minutes. Invert onto serving plate. Drizzle with mixture of confectioners' sugar and lemon juice. Yield: 16 servings.

Approx Per Serving: Cal 309; Prot 3 g; Carbo 51 g; Fiber <1 g;
      T Fat 11 g; Chol 53 mg; Sod 214 mg.

BANANA CAKE

1 2-layer package
   yellow cake mix
1 4-ounce package
   vanilla instant
   pudding mix

3/4 cup oil
4 eggs
1/2 cup water
4 bananas, mashed
1 1/2 cups chopped pecans

Combine cake mix, pudding mix, oil, eggs and water in mixer bowl; mix well. Stir in bananas and pecans. Spoon into greased and floured bundt pan. Bake at 350 degrees for 45 minutes. Cool in pan for several minutes. Invert onto serving plate. Yield: 16 servings.

Approx Per Serving: Cal 374; Prot 4 g; Carbo 42 g; Fiber 2 g;
      T Fat 22 g; Chol 53 mg; Sod 262 mg.

BLACK FOREST DUMP CAKE

1 20-ounce can crushed
pineapple
1 21-ounce can cherry
pie filling

1 2-layer package
devil's food cake mix
1 cup chopped pecans
1/2 cup melted margarine

Drain pineapple, reserving juice. Spread pineapple in lightly greased 9x13-inch cake pan. Spoon pie filling over pineapple. Sprinkle with dry cake mix and pecans. Combine melted margarine and reserved juice in bowl; mix well. Drizzle over layers. Bake at 350 degrees for 35 to 40 minutes or until brown. Cut this moist cake-like dessert into squares. Yield: 15 servings.

Approx Per Serving: Cal 321; Prot 2 g; Carbo 48 g; Fiber 1 g;
T Fat 14 g; Chol 0 mg; Sod 293 mg.

SURPRISE CARROT CAKE

1 2-layer package
yellow cake mix
1 1/2 cups mayonnaise-
type salad dressing

4 eggs
2 teaspoons cinnamon
2 cups shredded carrots
1/2 cup chopped walnuts

Combine cake mix, salad dressing, eggs and cinnamon in bowl; mix well. Stir in carrots and walnuts. Spoon into greased 9x13-inch cake pan. Bake at 350 degrees for 35 minutes. Cool on wire rack. Yield: 24 servings.

Approx Per Serving: Cal 182; Prot 3 g; Carbo 23 g; Fiber <1 g;
T Fat 9 g; Chol 39 mg; Sod 250 mg.

Brush or vacuum the condenser coils of the refrigerator at least twice a year for maximum energy efficiency.

GERMAN CHOCOLATE UPSIDE-DOWN CAKE

1 cup chopped pecans
1 cup coconut
1 2-layer package
German chocolate
cake mix

8 ounces cream cheese,
softened
1/2 cup margarine, softened
1 1-pound package
confectioners' sugar

Combine pecans and coconut in bowl. Sprinkle in greased 9x13-inch cake pan lined with greased waxed paper. Prepare cake mix using package directions. Spoon into prepared cake pan. Combine cream cheese and margarine in bowl; beat until smooth. Beat in confectioners' sugar. Spoon over cake batter. Bake at 325 degrees for 45 minutes. Cool in pan for 45 minutes. Cut into squares. Invert servings onto serving plates. Yield: 15 servings.

Approx Per Serving: Cal 570; Prot 5 g; Carbo 82 g; Fiber 1 g;
T Fat 27 g; Chol 17 mg; Sod 285 mg.

COCONUT CAKE

1 2-layer package white
cake mix
1 14-ounce can
sweetened condensed
milk

1 15-ounce can cream
of coconut
8 ounces whipped topping
1 8-ounce package
frozen coconut, thawed

Prepare and bake cake mix using package directions for 9x13-inch cake pan. Pierce holes in hot cake with fork. Pour mixture of condensed milk and cream of coconut over cake gradually. Let stand, covered, until cool. Spread with whipped topping; sprinkle with coconut. Store in refrigerator. Flavor improves overnight. Yield: 15 servings.

Approx Per Serving: Cal 549; Prot 7 g; Carbo 70 g; Fiber 2 g;
T Fat 29 g; Chol 9 mg; Sod 247 mg.

LEMON ANGEL DELIGHT CAKE

1 1-step package angel
food cake mix
1 21-ounce can lemon
pie filling
8 ounces cream cheese,
softened

1/2 cup margarine,
softened
1 1-pound package
confectioners' sugar
1 teaspoon vanilla extract

Combine cake mix and pie filling in mixer bowl; beat until smooth. Spread in ungreased 10x15-inch cake pan. Bake at 350 degrees for 20 to 25 minutes or until cake tests done. Cool to room temperature. Blend cream cheese and margarine in bowl. Add confectioners' sugar and vanilla; beat until smooth. Spread on cake. Cut into squares or roll as for jelly roll to enclose frosting. Yield: 24 servings.

Approx Per Serving: Cal 309; Prot 4 g; Carbo 58 g; Fiber <1 g;
T Fat 7 g; Chol 10 mg; Sod 199 mg.

PISTACHIO CAKE

1 3-ounce package
pistachio instant
pudding mix
1 2-layer package white
cake mix
4 eggs
1 cup club soda

1/4 cup oil
1/2 cup chopped pecans
1 1/2 cups cold milk
1 1/2 cups whipped topping
1 3-ounce package
pistachio pudding mix

Combine 1 package pudding mix, cake mix, eggs, soda and oil in mixer bowl; mix well. Beat for 4 minutes. Stir in pecans. Pour into greased and floured 9x13-inch cake pan. Bake at 350 degrees for 40 to 45 minutes or until cake tests done. Let stand until cool. Combine remaining ingredients in mixer bowl; mix until smooth. Spread over cake. Yield: 15 servings.

Approx Per Serving: Cal 307; Prot 4 g; Carbo 43 g; Fiber <1 g;
T Fat 13 g; Chol 60 mg; Sod 319 mg.

POPPY SEED CAKE

1 2-layer package lemon
  cake mix
1 4-ounce package
  vanilla instant
  pudding mix

3/4 cup oil
3/4 cup water
4 eggs
1 1-ounce jar poppy
  seed

Combine cake mix, pudding mix, oil, water and eggs in bowl; mix well. Stir in poppy seed. Spoon into greased and floured bundt pan. Bake at 350 degrees for 45 to 50 minutes or until cake tests done. Invert onto wire rack to cool. Yield: 24 servings.

Approx Per Serving: Cal 188; Prot 2 g; Carbo 23 g; Fiber <1 g;
    T Fat 10 g; Chol 36 mg; Sod 174 mg.

PRUNE CAKE

2 cups self-rising flour
2 cups sugar
1 teaspoon cinnamon
1/2 teaspoon cloves
1 cup oil

3 eggs
2 4-ounce jars baby
  food prunes
1 cup chopped pecans

Combine flour, sugar, cinnamon and cloves in large mixer bowl; mix well. Add oil, eggs and prunes; mix well. Stir in pecans. Spoon into greased and floured 9x13-inch cake pan. Bake at 325 degrees for 35 minutes or until wooden pick inserted in center comes out clean. Cover with foil immediately. Cake will be more moist if placed in freezer while still hot. May drizzle with favorite glaze. Yield: 15 servings.

Approx Per Serving: Cal 375; Prot 4 g; Carbo 45 g; Fiber 2 g;
    T Fat 21 g; Chol 43 mg; Sod 195 mg.

STRAWBERRY CAKE

1 2-layer package
   yellow cake mix
1 3-ounce package
   strawberry gelatin

1 16-ounce bottle of
   strawberry soda
8 ounces whipped topping
24 fresh strawberries

Prepare and bake cake mix using package directions for 9x13-inch cake pan. Cool in pan. Prepare gelatin using package directions, substituting strawberry soda for water. Chill until partially set. Punch holes in cake with handle of wooden spoon. Spoon gelatin over cake. Spread with whipped topping. Arrange strawberries over top. Chill for 4 hours or longer. Yield: 24 servings.

Approx Per Serving: Cal 211; Prot 2 g; Carbo 35 g; Fiber <1 g;
   T Fat 8 g; Chol 0 mg; Sod 121 mg.

BUTTERSCOTCH CLUSTERS

2 cups butterscotch chips
1 8-ounce can peanuts

1 5-ounce can chow
   mein noodles

Melt butterscotch chips in saucepan over low heat, stirring constantly. Stir in peanuts and noodles. Drop by spoonfuls onto waxed paper. Let stand until firm. Yield: 24 servings.

Approx Per Serving: Cal 155; Prot 4 g; Carbo 13 g; Fiber 2 g;
   T Fat 11 g; Chol 1 mg; Sod 63 mg.

Use clean, high quality heat reflectors under stove-top burners. This can save as much as 33 percent of the energy used when cooking on top of the stove.

FORGOTTEN TREATS

2 egg whites
2/3 cup sugar
1/8 teaspoon salt
1 teaspoon vinegar

1 teaspoon vanilla extract
1 cup chopped pecans
1 cup chocolate chips

Beat egg whites in mixer bowl until soft peaks form. Add sugar and salt gradually, beating until stiff peaks form. Add vinegar and vanilla; mix well. Fold in pecans and chocolate chips. Drop by teaspoonfuls onto baking sheets lined with baking parchment. Place in oven preheated to 350 degrees. Turn off oven. Let stand until cool. Yield: 40 servings.

Approx Per Serving: Cal 55; Prot 1 g; Carbo 6 g; Fiber <1 g;
    T Fat 4 g; Chol 0 mg; Sod 10 mg.

SLOW-COOKER FUDGE

1 cup butter
8 ounces Velveeta
  cheese, chopped
1 1/2 teaspoons vanilla
  extract

2 1-pound packages
   confectioners' sugar
1/2 cup baking cocoa
2 cups chopped pecans

Melt butter and cheese in slow-cooker on Low, stirring to mix well. Stir in vanilla. Sift confectioners' sugar and cocoa together. Add to cheese mixture gradually, mixing well after each addition. Stir in pecans. Pour into buttered 9x13-inch dish. Let stand until firm. Cut into squares. Yield: 120 servings.

Approx Per Serving: Cal 70; Prot 1 g; Carbo 10 g; Fiber <1 g;
    T Fat 4 g; Chol 6 mg; Sod 40 mg.

 Every time you open the oven door, you lose 25 to 50 degrees of heat.

PEANUT BUTTER FUDGE

1 1-pound package
   confectioners' sugar
1/2 cup peanut butter
1/2 cup baking cocoa

2 teaspoons vanilla
   extract
Salt to taste
1 cup margarine, softened

Combine confectioners' sugar, peanut butter, cocoa, vanilla and salt in bowl; mix well. Spread in buttered 9x9-inch dish. Let stand until firm. Cut into squares. Yield: 36 servings.

Approx Per Serving: Cal 283; Prot 1 g; Carbo 16 g; Fiber 1 g;
T Fat 24 g; Chol 0 mg; Sod 205 mg.

MINT DROPS

2 cups confectioners'
   sugar
2 tablespoons cream
   cheese, softened

1 teaspoon peppermint
   extract

Combine confectioners' sugar, cream cheese and flavoring in bowl; mix well. Roll on flat surface. Cut into desired shapes. Chill in refrigerator. Yield: 24 servings.

Approx Per Serving: Cal 43; Prot <1 g; Carbo 10 g; Fiber 0 g;
T Fat <1 g; Chol 2 mg; Sod 4 mg.

PEANUT BUTTER BALLS

1/2 cup confectioners'
   sugar
1/2 cup sweetened
   condensed milk

1 cup peanut butter
1/2 cup confectioners'
   sugar

Combine 1/2 cup confectioners' sugar, condensed milk and peanut butter in bowl; mix well. Shape into small balls. Roll in 1/2 cup confectioners' sugar, coating well. Store in airtight container. Yield: 32 servings.

Approx Per Serving: Cal 70; Prot 3 g; Carbo 6 g; Fiber 1 g;
T Fat 5 g; Chol 2 mg; Sod 39 mg.

PEOPLE PUPPY CHOW

1/2 cup margarine
1 cup peanut butter
2 cups miniature
   semisweet chocolate
   chips

1 15-ounce package
   Crispix cereal
4 cups confectioners'
   sugar

Melt margarine, peanut butter and chocolate chips in saucepan over low heat, stirring to mix well. Pour over cereal in large bowl; mix gently to coat well. Place confectioners' sugar in large bag. Add cereal mixture 1/4 at a time, shaking to coat well. Spread on tray to dry and cool. Store in airtight container. Yield: 30 servings.

Approx Per Serving: Cal 253; Prot 4 g; Carbo 36 g; Fiber 1 g;
   T Fat 12 g; Chol 0 mg; Sod 199 mg.

QUICK CANDY

2 cups miniature
   marshmallows
2 1/2 cups Captain Crunch
   cereal

2 cups crisp rice cereal
2 cups dry-roasted
   peanuts
2 pounds white chocolate

Combine marshmallows, cereal and peanuts in bowl; mix well. Melt white chocolate in saucepan over low heat, stirring constantly. Pour over cereal mixture; mix well. Drop by spoonfuls onto waxed paper. Let stand until cool. Yield: 72 servings.

Approx Per Serving: Cal 101; Prot 2 g; Carbo 11 g; Fiber 1 g;
   T Fat 6 g; Chol 3 mg; Sod 38 mg.

 Do not preheat oven longer than necessary; ten minutes should be sufficient.

REESE BARS

3/4 cup melted margarine
1 cup peanut butter
1 1-pound package
    confectioners' sugar

1 8-ounce milk
    chocolate bar, melted

Combine margarine and peanut butter in medium bowl; mix well. Stir in confectioners' sugar. Spread in 9x13-inch dish. Spread chocolate evenly over top. Let stand until firm. Cut into bars. Yield: 40 servings.

Approx Per Serving: Cal 150; Prot 2 g; Carbo 18 g; Fiber 1 g;
    T Fat 9 g; Chol 1 mg; Sod 71 mg.

TRUFFLES

2 pounds pecans
18 ounces milk chocolate
1 14-ounce can
    sweetened condensed
    milk

1 7-ounce jar
    marshmallow creme
40 marshmallows

Chop pecans coarsely. Break chocolate into pieces. Combine chocolate, condensed milk and marshmallow creme in double boiler. Cook over low heat until chocolate is melted, stirring frequently with wooden spoon. Cool for 5 to 10 minutes, stirring frequently. Dip each marshmallow into chocolate mixture with fork. Roll in pecans, coating well. Place on waxed paper, reshaping and rolling again in pecans if necessary. Place on foil-lined baking sheet. Chill in refrigerator or freezer until firm. Yield: 40 servings.

Approx Per Serving: Cal 286; Prot 4 g; Carbo 27 g; Fiber 2 g;
    T Fat 20 g; Chol 6 mg; Sod 32 mg.

CRISP CARAMEL TREATS

¹/₄ cup margarine	5 cups crisp rice cereal
4 cups miniature marshmallows	2 caramel sheets

Melt margarine in saucepan over low heat. Add marshmallows and cereal; mix well. Press half the mixture into 9x9-inch pan. Top with caramel sheets, pressing lightly to cover well. Top with remaining cereal mixture, pressing lightly. Cool completely. Cut into squares. Caramel sheets are sold for making caramel apples. Yield: 16 servings.

Approx Per Serving: Cal 105; Prot 1 g; Carbo 19 g; Fiber <1 g;
T Fat 3 g; Chol 0 mg; Sod 152 mg.
Nutritional information does not include caramel sheets.

EASY BROWN SUGAR BARS

1 1-pound package light brown sugar	4 eggs, beaten
2 cups baking mix	2 cups chopped pecans

Combine brown sugar, baking mix, eggs and pecans in bowl; mix well. Spread in greased and floured 9x13-inch baking pan. Bake at 325 degrees for 30 to 35 minutes or until firm. Cool on wire rack; cut into bars. Garnish with confectioners' sugar. Yield: 48 servings.

Approx Per Serving: Cal 98; Prot 1 g; Carbo 14 g; Fiber <1 g;
T Fat 5 g; Chol 18 mg; Sod 76 mg.

 Reduce energy consumption by 15 percent by using the dishwasher air-dry setting instead of the heat-dry setting.

CHESS SQUARES

¹/₂ cup melted margarine
1 2-layer package
  yellow cake mix
1 egg
1 1-pound package
  confectioners' sugar

2 eggs, beaten
8 ounces cream cheese,
  softened

Combine margarine, cake mix and 1 egg in mixer bowl; mix well. Press into 9x13-inch dish. Combine confectioners' sugar, 2 eggs and cream cheese in mixer bowl; mix until smooth. Spread over cake mix layer. Bake at 325 degrees for 40 minutes. Cool on wire rack. Cut into squares. Yield: 36 servings.

Approx Per Serving: Cal 170; Prot 2 g; Carbo 27 g; Fiber 0 g; T Fat 6 g; Chol 25 mg; Sod 142 mg.

CHOCOLATE CHIP BROWNIES

1 20-ounce roll
  chocolate chip
  cookie dough
3 eggs

1 cup sugar
24 ounces cream cheese,
  softened

Cut cookie dough roll into halves lengthwise. Cut each half into slices. Arrange half the slices in greased and floured 9x13-inch baking pan. Beat eggs, sugar and cream cheese in bowl until smooth. Spoon over cookie dough. Top with remaining cookie dough; slices will not overlap. Bake at 375 degrees for 40 to 45 minutes or until golden brown. Cut into squares. Serve warm with vanilla ice cream. Yield: 16 servings.

Approx Per Serving: Cal 377; Prot 6 g; Carbo 37 g; Fiber 1 g; T Fat 24 g; Chol 103 mg; Sod 267 mg.

CHOCOLATE CHIP COOKIES

1 2-layer package white
   cake mix
3/4 cup oil

1 cup semisweet
   chocolate chips
1 egg

Combine cake mix, oil, chocolate chips and egg in bowl; mix well. Shape into small balls. Place on ungreased cookie sheet. Bake at 350 degrees for 6 to 8 minutes or until soft set. Bake longer for crisper cookies. May add 1/2 cup chopped pecans and 1/4 cup light brown sugar or use butter-scotch chips and yellow cake mix. Yield: 36 servings.

Approx Per Serving: Cal 127; Prot 1 g; Carbo 15 g; Fiber <1 g;
   T Fat 8 g; Chol 6 mg; Sod 90 mg.

TOLL HOUSE PAN COOKIES

1 cup butter, softened
3/4 cup sugar
3/4 cup packed brown
   sugar
1 teaspoon vanilla extract
2 eggs

2¹/4 cups flour
1 teaspoon soda
1 teaspoon salt
2 cups semisweet
   chocolate chips
1 cup chopped pecans

Cream butter, sugar, brown sugar and vanilla in mixer bowl until light and fluffy. Beat in eggs. Add mixture of flour, soda and salt gradually; mix well. Stir in chocolate chips and pecans. Spread in greased 10x15-inch baking pan. Bake at 375 degrees for 20 minutes. Cool on wire rack. Cut into 2-inch squares. Yield: 35 servings.

Approx Per Serving: Cal 187; Prot 2 g; Carbo 21 g; Fiber 1 g;
   T Fat 11 g; Chol 26 mg; Sod 136 mg.

CANDIED FRUIT COOKIES

2 cups graham cracker
  crumbs
1 cup chopped candied
  fruit

1 cup chopped pecans
1 14-ounce can
  sweetened condensed
  milk

Combine cracker crumbs, candied fruit, pecans and condensed milk in bowl; mix well. Drop by teaspoonfuls 1 inch apart onto greased and floured cookie sheet. Bake at 325 degrees for 12 minutes. Remove immediately to wire rack to cool. Yield: 60 servings.

Approx Per Serving: Cal 58; Prot 1 g; Carbo 9 g; Fiber <1 g;
  T Fat 2 g; Chol 2 mg; Sod 33 mg.

LEMON SNAPS

1 2-layer package lemon
  cake mix
2 cups whipped topping

1 egg, beaten
1/2 cup sifted
  confectioners' sugar

Combine cake mix, whipped topping and egg in bowl; mix well. Drop by teaspoonfuls into confectioners' sugar; roll to coat well. Place 1 1/2 inches apart on greased cookie sheet. Bake at 350 degrees for 10 to 15 minutes or until golden brown. Remove to wire rack to cool.
Yield: 48 servings.

Approx Per Serving: Cal 62; Prot 1 g; Carbo 11 g; Fiber 0 g;
  T Fat 2 g; Chol 4 mg; Sod 68 mg.

OATMEAL COOKIES

1 cup packed brown
  sugar
1 cup sugar
1¹/₂ cups flour
1 teaspoon soda
¹/₂ teaspoon cinnamon

¹/₂ teaspoon ginger
¹/₂ teaspoon salt
1 cup oil
2 eggs
1 teaspoon vanilla extract
3 cups oats

Combine brown sugar, sugar, flour, soda, cinnamon, ginger and salt in bowl; mix well. Add oil, eggs and vanilla; beat until smooth. Stir in oats. Drop by teaspoonfuls onto greased cookie sheet. Bake at 350 degrees for 10 to 12 minutes or until light brown. Remove to wire rack to cool. Yield: 48 servings.

Approx Per Serving: Cal 111; Prot 1 g; Carbo 15 g; Fiber 1 g;
    T Fat 5 g; Chol 9 mg; Sod 45 mg.

EASY PEANUT BUTTER COOKIES

1 cup sugar
1 cup peanut butter

1 egg
1 teaspoon vanilla extract

Combine sugar, peanut butter, egg and vanilla in bowl; mix well. Drop by teaspoonfuls onto greased baking sheet. Bake at 350 degrees for 10 minutes. Remove to wire rack to cool. Yield: 24 servings.

Approx Per Serving: Cal 100; Prot 3 g; Carbo 10 g; Fiber 1 g;
    T Fat 6 g; Chol 9 mg; Sod 46 mg.

SEVEN-LAYER WOW BARS

1/4 cup butter
1 1/2 cup graham cracker
  crumbs
1 cup coconut
1 cup chocolate chips

1 cup butterscotch chips
1 14-ounce can
  sweetened condensed
  milk
1 cup chopped pecans

Melt butter in 9x13-inch baking dish. Layer cracker crumbs, coconut, chocolate chips, butterscotch chips and condensed milk in prepared pan. Sprinkle with pecans. Bake at 325 degrees for 30 minutes. Cool on wire rack. Cut into squares. Yield: 32 servings.

Approx Per Serving: Cal 164; Prot 2 g; Carbo 18 g; Fiber 1 g;
  T Fat 10 g; Chol 12 mg; Sod 65 mg.

SUGAR COOKIES

1 cup margarine, softened
2 cups sugar
2 eggs
1/2 teaspoon vanilla
  extract

3 cups flour
1 tablespoon cream of
  tartar
1 teaspoon soda

Cream margarine and sugar in mixer bowl until light and fluffy. Beat in eggs and vanilla. Mix flour, cream of tartar and soda together. Add to creamed mixture, mixing well. Chill, covered, for several hours. Shape into small balls. Place on lightly greased cookie sheet. Bake at 350 degrees for 10 minutes. Remove to wire rack to cool. Yield: 24 servings.

Approx Per Serving: Cal 196; Prot 2 g; Carbo 29 g; Fiber <1 g;
  T Fat 8 g; Chol 18 mg; Sod 130 mg.

WHITE ALMOND BARS

4 eggs
2 cups sugar
1/4 teaspoon salt
2 cups flour
1 cup melted margarine

2 teaspoons almond
   flavoring
1/4 cup sugar
1 cup slivered almonds

Beat eggs, 2 cups sugar and salt in bowl until thick and lemon-colored. Mix flour and margarine in bowl. Add to egg mixture; mix well. Stir in flavoring. Spoon into greased and floured 9x13-inch baking pan. Sprinkle with 1/4 cup sugar and almonds. Bake at 325 degrees for 30 minutes. Yield: 36 servings.

Approx Per Serving: Cal 150; Prot 2 g; Carbo 19 g; Fiber 1 g;
   T Fat 8 g; Chol 24 mg; Sod 83 mg.

APPLE YOGURT PIE

3 1/2 pounds apples,
   peeled, thinly sliced
1 unbaked 9-inch pie shell
1/2 cup sugar

1 teaspoon cinnamon
1 egg
1 cup plain yogurt

Spread apples in pie shell; sprinkle with sugar and cinnamon. Bake at 425 degrees for 15 minutes. Beat egg with yogurt in bowl. Spoon over apples. Bake for 30 minutes longer. Garnish hot pie with sprinkle of additional cinnamon and sugar. Serve warm. Yield: 8 servings.

Approx Per Serving: Cal 307; Prot 4 g; Carbo 54 g; Fiber 5 g;
   T Fat 9 g; Chol 28 mg; Sod 168 mg.

CHERRY CHEESE PIE

8 ounces cream cheese,
softened
1 14-ounce can
sweetened condensed
milk
¹/₃ cup lemon juice

1 teaspoon vanilla extract
1 9-inch graham cracker
pie shell
1 21-ounce can cherry
pie filling, chilled

Beat cream cheese in mixer bowl until light and fluffy. Add condensed milk; mix until smooth. Stir in lemon juice and vanilla. Spoon into pie shell. Chill for 3 hours or longer. Spoon pie filling evenly over top. May substitute blueberry pie filling for cherry. Yield: 8 servings.

Approx Per Serving: Cal 537; Prot 8 g; Carbo 73 g; Fiber 2 g;
T Fat 25 g; Chol 48 mg; Sod 408 mg.

CHESS PIE

¹/₂ cup butter
1¹/₂ cups sugar
3 eggs, beaten
1 tablespoon vanilla
extract

1 tablespoon cider
vinegar
¹/₄ teaspoon salt
1 unbaked 8-inch pie shell

Combine butter and sugar in saucepan. Heat until butter melts, stirring constantly; remove from heat. Mix in eggs. Stir in vanilla, vinegar and salt. Pour into pie shell. Bake at 300 degrees for 50 minutes or until set and golden brown. Yield: 8 servings.

Approx Per Serving: Cal 394; Prot 4 g; Carbo 48 g; Fiber <1 g;
T Fat 21 g; Chol 111 mg; Sod 328 mg.

CHOCOLATE CHIP PIES

1 cup sugar
1 cup packed brown
  sugar
1/2 cup melted margarine
4 eggs, beaten

1 cup chopped pecans
1 cup chocolate chips
2 unbaked 9-inch pie
  shells

Combine sugar, brown sugar, margarine and eggs in bowl; mix well. Stir in pecans and chocolate chips. Spoon into pie shells. Bake at 350 degrees for 40 minutes. Yield: 16 servings.

Approx Per Serving: Cal 386; Prot 4 g; Carbo 43 g; Fiber 1 g;
    T Fat 23 g; Chol 53 mg; Sod 230 mg.

FUDGE PIE

1/4 cup margarine
1 1/2 cups sugar
1/4 cup baking cocoa
2 eggs

1 teaspoon vanilla extract
1 6-ounce can
  evaporated milk
1 unbaked 9-inch pie shell

Melt margarine in saucepan. Add sugar, cocoa, eggs, vanilla and evaporated milk in order listed, mixing well after each addition. Pour into pie shell. Bake at 300 degrees for 1 hour. Serve with whipped topping or ice cream. Yield: 8 servings.

Approx Per Serving: Cal 365; Prot 5 g; Carbo 51 g; Fiber 1 g;
    T Fat 17 g; Chol 60 mg; Sod 246 mg.

IMPOSSIBLE COCONUT PIE

2 eggs, beaten
1 cup sugar
1/4 cup self-rising flour
2 tablespoons margarine,
  softened

1 cup milk
1/2 teaspoon vanilla
  extract
1 31/2-ounce can flaked
  coconut

Combine eggs, sugar, flour and margarine in bowl; mix well. Add milk and vanilla; mix well. Stir in coconut. Pour into greased 9-inch pie plate. Bake at 350 degrees for 30 minutes. Pie will make its own crust. Yield: 8 servings.

Approx Per Serving: Cal 230; Prot 3 g; Carbo 35 g; Fiber 2 g;
  T Fat 9 g; Chol 57 mg; Sod 109 mg.

LEMONADE PIES

1 6-ounce can frozen
  lemonade concentrate,
  thawed
12 ounces whipped
  topping

1 14-ounce can
  sweetened condensed
  milk
2 9-inch graham cracker
  pie shells

Combine lemonade concentrate, whipped topping and condensed milk in bowl; mix well. Spoon into pie shells. Chill, covered, until firm. Yield: 12 servings.

Approx Per Serving: Cal 495; Prot 5 g; Carbo 65 g; Fiber 1 g;
  T Fat 25 g; Chol 11 mg; Sod 368 mg.

FROZEN PEANUT BUTTER PIE

3/4 cup sifted
  confectioners' sugar
3 ounces cream cheese,
  softened
1/2 cup peanut butter
2 tablespoons milk

8 ounces whipped
  topping
1 9-inch chocolate
  crumb pie shell
1/4 cup chopped peanuts

Cream confectioners' sugar and cream cheese in mixer bowl until light and fluffy. Add peanut butter and milk; beat until smooth. Fold in whipped topping. Spoon into pie shell. Sprinkle with peanuts. Freeze until firm. Serve frozen. Yield: 8 servings.

Approx Per Serving: Cal 492; Prot 9 g; Carbo 45 g; Fiber 2 g; T Fat 32 g; Chol 12 mg; Sod 345 mg.

EASY PECAN PIES

1/2 cup melted margarine
1 1-pound package light
  brown sugar
3 eggs
1/2 cup evaporated milk

1 teaspoon vanilla extract
1/2 cup chopped pecans
2 unbaked 9-inch pie
  shells

Combine margarine and brown sugar in bowl; mix well. Stir in eggs, evaporated milk, vanilla and pecans. Spoon into pie shells. Bake at 350 degrees for 45 minutes or until set. Yield: 16 servings.

Approx Per Serving: Cal 320; Prot 4 g; Carbo 39 g; Fiber <1 g; T Fat 27 g; Chol 43 mg; Sod 239 mg.

PEPPERMINT ICE CREAM PIE

1½ cups chocolate wafer
  crumbs
6 tablespoons melted
  butter
1 pint peppermint ice
  cream, softened

8 ounces whipped
  topping
3 tablespoons finely
  crushed peppermint
  candy

Combine chocolate wafer crumbs and butter in bowl; mix well. Press over bottom and side of 9-inch pie plate. Combine ice cream and whipped topping in bowl; mix until smooth. Spoon into pie shell. Sprinkle with crushed candy. Freeze until firm. Garnish with additional crushed candy if desired. Yield: 8 servings.

Approx Per Serving: Cal 455; Prot 4 g; Carbo 49 g; Fiber <1 g;
  T Fat 28 g; Chol 38 mg; Sod 311 mg.

PINEAPPLE REFRIGERATOR PIES

1 14-ounce can
  sweetened condensed
  milk
Juice of 1 lemon
1 20-ounce can crushed
  pineapple, drained

8 ounces whipped
  topping
1 cup chopped walnuts
2 9-inch graham cracker
  pie shells

Combine condensed milk and lemon juice in bowl; mix well. Stir in pineapple. Fold in whipped topping and walnuts. Spoon into pie shells. Chill until serving time. Yield: 16 servings.

Approx Per Serving: Cal 397; Prot 5 g; Carbo 49 g; Fiber 2 g;
  T Fat 21 g; Chol 8 mg; Sod 275 mg.

PUMPKIN PIE

1/2 cup packed brown
  sugar
8 ounces cream cheese,
  softened
2 eggs

2/3 cup canned pumpkin
3/4 teaspoon pumpkin pie
  spice
1 8-inch graham cracker
  pie shell

Cream brown sugar and cream cheese in mixer bowl until light and fluffy. Beat in eggs. Add pumpkin and spice; mix well. Spoon into pie shell. Bake at 350 degrees for 35 minutes. Cool to room temperature. Chill until serving time. Yield: 8 servings.

Approx Per Serving: Cal 381; Prot 6 g; Carbo 41 g; Fiber 1 g;
    T Fat 22 g; Chol 84 mg; Sod 347 mg.

STRAWBERRY PIE

3 tablespoons strawberry
  gelatin
3 tablespoons flour
1 cup sugar

1 cup water
1 quart strawberries
1 baked 9-inch pie shell

Combine gelatin, flour and sugar in saucepan. Stir in water. Bring to a boil, stirring to dissolve gelatin and sugar completely. Remove from heat. Place strawberries in pie shell. Pour gelatin mixture over top. Chill until firm. Garnish with whipped topping. Yield: 8 servings.

Approx Per Serving: Cal 262; Prot 3 g; Carbo 47 g; Fiber 2 g;
    T Fat 8 g; Chol 0 mg; Sod 156 mg.

Microwave Magic

Microwave Guides

One of the most efficient appliances in the kitchen is the microwave. It has the double advantage of speed and energy conservation. Most things cook in the microwave in less than half the time of a conventional oven and expend much less energy. It requires, for example, almost nine times as much energy to cook four hamburger patties in the oven as in the microwave. And, since microwaves move through air and dishes, only the food gets hot. The kitchen stays cool and the only heat in the oven or dish comes from the hot food.

Microwave Cookware

There are many kinds of cookware that are safe for microwave use. Many department stores have an extensive display of special microwave cookware, which is, of course, the very best choice. However, with the following guidelines, you can improvise.

- **China, pottery**—Ideal for microwave cooking, if there is no metallic trim or glaze
- **Glass**—Nearly always safe
- **Paper**—Use only for short cooking or reheating
- **Plastic**—Use only plastics that are dishwasher safe, and only for short cooking or reheating; do not use for foods with high fat or sugar content
- **Plastic cooking pouches**—Use only if tied loosely with string; metal twist ties may cause bags to melt; slit the pouch to allow steam to escape
- **Straw, wood**—May be used only for very quick warming; be certain there is no metal used as fasteners

To test a container for microwave safety, place a glass measuring cup containing one cup water on the container you wish to test. Microwave on High for one minute. If the container feels hot, it should not be used in the microwave oven. If it feels warm, it may be used only for warming foods. If the dish has remained at room temperature, it is microproof and may be used for any microwave cooking.

Microwave Power Levels

The most important factor in preparing recipes other than those provided by the manufacturer of your microwave is determining the correct power level and time for your <u>particular</u> oven. The recipes in this chapter have been formulated for a microwave which operates on 650 to 700 watts power on High. Many of the smaller microwaves operate on as little as 450 to 500 watts on High.

If you have a less powerful microwave, you must add additional time to the recipes. For example, if your microwave operates on 500 watts on High, multiply the amount of cooking time by 1.3 in order to estimate the cooking time you actually will need. A casserole requiring 10 minutes in a 700-watt microwave may require 13 minutes in a 500-watt oven. The following chart is a guideline for using the power levels of a 650 to 700-watt microwave.

% Power	Power Setting	Use For
100	High	Tender cuts of meat, poultry, fish, vegetables and casseroles
90	Sauté	Onions, celery, green peppers; reheating sliced meats
80	Reheat	Reheat prepared foods
70	Roast	Melting butter and chocolate; rump roasts, ham, veal and lamb; cheese and egg dishes and meat loaf
60	Bake	Start quick breads to finish on High
50	Simmer	Sauces, stews, soup
40	Braise	Less tender cuts of meat cooked in liquid; custards
30	Defrost	Thawing meats, poultry and seafood; cooking pasta
20	Low	Softening chocolate and butter; heating rolls, breads, pancakes and French toast
10	Warm	Softening cream cheese; raising bread dough; keeping casseroles and main dishes warm

Microwave Time Factors

There are several factors in addition to power level which will affect the cooking time of food in a microwave oven. These need to be taken into account.

- **Quantity of food**. More food means more time. While a single potato cooks in four minutes, additional potatoes increase cooking time dramatically. Never vary the quantities in a recipe without taking into consideration that the time will change.
- **Temperature of food**. More time is needed for cooking cold foods because more energy must be absorbed to heat them.
- **Moisture content of food**. Fresh foods with lots of moisture cook faster than drier foods.
- **Standing time**. Food continues to cook during the standing time.

Microwave Techniques

Many microwave cooking techniques are standard to all cooking while others are unique to microwaving. These are necessary to compensate for uneven energy distribution in many microwaves.

- **Covering**. Covering holds in the steam and helps foods cook faster.
- **Stirring**. Stirring redistributes the heat but only needs to be done occasionally.
- **Turning over or rearranging**. This moves large pieces of meat or vegetables into a different energy pattern to ensure even cooking.
- **Arranging**. Arranging several items in a ring with space between them leaves the center open so energy can penetrate from all sides.
- **Shielding**. This protects areas such as a turkey breast bone which absorb the most energy from overcooking. Use small strips of foil.
- **Rotating**. This allows foods such as lasagna which cannot be stirred to heat evenly. Dishes should be given a one-quarter turn.

Microwave Charts

These charts are a handy reference guide for defrosting and cooking main dish meats, poultry, seafood and vegetables. Microwave defrosting warms and thaws food without cooking it. Standing time is a very important part of the defrosting cycle.

Meat—Poultry—Seafood

When meat is removed from the microwave, it will be icy in the center. If you thaw the meat entirely in the microwave the edges begin to cook. Most items need to stand only for about the same amount of time they have been defrosted. **Let meats stand for 10 minutes or longer after cooking to complete the cooking cycle.**

Meat		Defrosting & Standing Time per pound (Medium-Low)	Cooking Time per pound (High)
Beef	Steak	6-8 minutes	6-8 minutes
	Roast	4-8 minutes (Let stand 1 hour or more)	5-5½ minutes (Rare) 6-6½ minutes (Medium) 7-8 minutes (Well)
	Ground Beef	5-6 minutes	5-6 minutes
Ham	Sliced, Half Whole Ham	5-6 minutes	8-10 minutes (Fresh) 5-6 minutes (Precooked)
Lamb	Chops	4-6 minutes	8-9 minutes
	Leg	5-7 minutes	9-11 minutes
	Shoulder	4-6 minutes	9-10 minutes
Pork	Chops	4-6 minutes	8-10 minutes
	Roast	4-5 minutes	8-10 minutes
	Sausage	4-6 minutes	10-12 minutes
	Spareribs	5-7 minutes	9-12 minutes
Veal	Chops	4-6 minutes	4-6 minutes
	Cutlets	4-6 minutes	4-6 minutes
	Roast	5-7 minutes	20-25 minutes

Poultry and Seafood		Defrosting & Standing Time per pound (Medium-Low)	Cooking Time per pound (High)
Poultry	Chicken	5-8 minutes	6-7 minutes
	Turkey	3-5 minutes	11-12 minutes
Fish	Filets	6-8 minutes	6-7 minutes
	Steaks	5-6 minutes	5-6 minutes
	Whole Fish	3-5 minutes	10-12 minutes
Shellfish	Clams (shucked)	3-5 minutes	3-4 minutes
	Lobster (cooked)	3-5 minutes	2-3 minutes
	Lobster (tails)	5-6 minutes	4-6 minutes
	Oysters (cooked)	3-5 minutes	2-4 minutes
	Oysters (shucked)	4-6 minutes	3-5 minutes
	Scallops	5-6 minutes	5-7 minutes
	Shrimp (cooked)	3-5 minutes	4-5 minutes

Fresh Vegetables

Vegetable	Amount	Procedure for Cooking	Time
Artichoke	4 medium	In a 3-quart covered casserole combine 1 cup water, 1/2 teaspoon salt and artichokes. Rotate dish 1/2 turn after 7 minutes.	14-15 minutes
Asparagus	16 (4-inch) pieces	In a 1 1/2-quart covered casserole combine 1/2 cup water, 1/2 teaspoon salt and asparagus. Stir halfway through cooking.	6-9 minutes
Beans wax	1 pound 1-inch pieces	In a 1 1/2-quart covered casserole combine 1/2 cup water, 1/2 teaspoon salt and beans. Stir halfway through cooking.	9-11 minutes
green	1 pound 1-inch pieces	Same procedure as above except increase water to 3/4 cup.	15-20 minutes
lima	2 pounds	Same as above.	7-8 minutes
Beets	4 medium, whole	In a 1 1/2-quart covered casserole combine 1/2 cup water, 1/2 teaspoon salt and beets. Stir halfway through cooking.	15-17 minutes

Vegetable	Amount	Procedure for Cooking	Time
Beets	4 medium, sliced or cubed	In a 1½-quart covered casserole combine ½ cup water, ½ teaspoon salt and beets. Stir halfway through cooking.	7-10 minutes
Broccoli	1 medium bunch	In a 1½-quart covered casserole combine ½ cup water, ½ teaspoon salt and broccoli.	8-10 minutes
Cabbage	1 medium head	In a 1½-quart covered casserole combine ½ cup water, ½ teaspoon salt and cabbage.	8-10 minutes
Carrots	6-8 sticks	In a 2-quart covered casserole combine ¼ cup water, ½ teaspoon salt and carrots. Stir halfway through cooking.	10-15 minutes
Cauliflower	1 medium head	In a 1½-quart covered casserole add ½ cup water, ½ teaspoon salt and cauliflower.	10-12 minutes
Corn	2 ears	Wrap ears in plastic wrap and place on oven shelf. Turn ears over halfway through cooking.	4-6 minutes
	4 ears	Same as above.	6-8 minutes
Eggplant	1 (14 to 16 ounce) whole, not pared	Wrap pierced eggplant in plastic wrap and place on oven shelf. Turn halfway through cooking.	8-10 minutes
Onions	4 medium, quartered	Place in covered casserole. Stir halfway through cooking.	11-13 minutes
Peas	2 pounds, shelled	In a 1½-quart covered casserole combine ¼ cup water, ¼ teaspoon salt and peas. Stir halfway through cooking.	7-10 minutes
Spinach	1 pound	Place spinach in a 2-quart covered casserole. Stir halfway through cooking.	6-8 minutes
Squash summer	1 pound, sliced or cubed	In a 1½-quart covered casserole combine ¼ cup water, ½ teaspoon salt, 2 tablespoons butter and squash.	10-14 minutes
Zucchini	1 pound, sliced or cubed	In a 1½-quart covered casserole combine ¼ cup water, ½ teaspoon salt, 2 tablespoons butter and zucchini.	10-14 minutes

Frozen Vegetables

Vegetable	Quantity	Utensil	Instructions	Time
Asparagus	10 ounces	1-quart glass casserole	Separate after 3 minutes. Casserole should be covered.	5-6 minutes
Broccoli	10 ounces	1-quart glass casserole	Separate after 4 minutes. Casserole should be covered.	8-9 minutes
Beans, green, cut or wax, French cut	10 ounces	1-quart glass casserole	Add 2 teaspoons hot water; stir. Cover.	7-8 minutes
Beans, lima fordhook	10 ounces	1-quart glass casserole	Add 1/4 cup water; stir after 5 minutes. Casserole should be covered.	7-8 minutes
Cauliflower	10 ounces	1-quart glass casserole	Add 2 tablespoons hot water; cover.	5-6 minutes
Corn, cut	10 ounces	1-quart glass casserole	Add 1/4 cup water; cover.	4-5 minutes
Corn	2 ears	1-quart glass casserole	Add 1/4 cup water; turn ears after 3 minutes. Cover.	5-6 minutes
Mixed Vegetables	10 ounces	1-quart glass casserole	Add 1/4 cup water; cover.	6-7 minutes
Okra	10 ounces	1-quart glass casserole	Add 2 tablespoons hot water; cover.	6-7 minutes
Peas, green	10 ounces	1-quart glass casserole	Add 2 tablespoons hot water; cover.	4-5 minutes
Peas & Carrots	10 ounces	1-quart glass casserole	Add 2 tablespoons hot water; cover. Stir after 3 minutes.	5-6 minutes
Spinach	10 ounces	1-quart glass casserole	Use covered casserole.	4-5 minutes

CHEESY CREAM OF BROCCOLI SOUP

1 10-ounce package
   frozen chopped broccoli
2 cups chopped celery
1 cup minced onion
1 cup cream-style
   cottage cheese

2 cups milk
1 10-ounce can cream
   of chicken soup
Salt and pepper to taste

Mix broccoli, celery and onion in 2^1/$_2$-quart glass dish. Microwave on High for 6 minutes, stirring once. Process cottage cheese in blender until smooth. Add milk and soup gradually, processing until smooth. Stir into broccoli mixture. Microwave on High for 3 minutes or until heated to serving temperature. Do not boil. Add salt and pepper.
Yield: 6 servings.

Approx Per Serving: Cal 158; Prot 10 g; Carbo 14 g; Fiber 3 g;
   T Fat 7 g; Chol 20 mg; Sod 594 mg.

HOT ITALIAN DIP

1 pound ground beef
^{1}/$_2$ cup chopped onion
1 clove of garlic, crushed
1 8-ounce can tomato
   sauce

^{1}/$_4$ cup catsup
1 teaspoon oregano
8 ounces cream cheese,
   chopped
^{1}/$_2$ cup Parmesan cheese

Crumble ground beef into plastic colander. Add onion and garlic. Place colander in glass bowl. Microwave on High for 4 to 6 minutes or until ground beef is no longer pink, stirring once. Discard drippings. Mix ground beef mixture with tomato sauce, catsup and oregano in glass dish. Microwave on High for 5 minutes. Add cream cheese. Microwave on Medium for 4 to 5 minutes or until cheese melts, stirring once. Stir in Parmesan cheese. Serve hot with rye bread or crackers. Yield: 12 servings.

Approx Per Serving: Cal 172; Prot 10 g; Carbo 4 g; Fiber <1 g;
   T Fat 13 g; Chol 48 mg; Sod 314 mg.

CHILI CON CARNE

1 cup chopped onion
1/2 cup chopped green
  bell pepper
1 pound ground beef
1 16-ounce can
  tomatoes
1/3 cup catsup

1 8-ounce can tomato
  sauce
1 16-ounce can chili
  beans
1 teaspoon salt
Chili powder and cayenne
  pepper to taste

Combine onion, green pepper and ground beef in 3-quart glass dish. Microwave on High for 12 minutes or until ground beef is no longer pink, stirring twice; drain. Add remaining ingredients; mix well. Microwave on Medium-High for 16 minutes or until heated through. Yield: 4 servings.

Approx Per Serving: Cal 402; Prot 30 g; Carbo 35 g; Fiber 12 g;
    T Fat 17 g; Chol 74 mg; Sod 1755 mg.

ROLLED ENCHILADAS

2 pounds ground beef
1/2 cup chopped onion
1 envelope taco
  seasoning mix
1/2 cup water
1 can refried beans
12 corn tortillas
1 8-ounce jar taco sauce

1 8-ounce can tomato
  sauce
2 cups shredded
  Cheddar cheese
4 cups shredded lettuce
1 large tomato, chopped
1 cup shredded Cheddar
  cheese

Brown ground beef in skillet; drain. Add onion, seasoning mix, water and refried beans; mix well. Simmer for 5 minutes. Spoon onto tortillas; roll to enclose filling. Place seam side down in greased 9x13-inch glass baking dish. Mix taco sauce and tomato sauce in bowl. Spoon over tortillas. Sprinkle with 2 cups cheese. Microwave on High for 10 minutes. Sprinkle with remaining ingredients. Yield: 12 servings.

Approx Per Serving: Cal 407; Prot 27 g; Carbo 27 g; Fiber 7 g;
    T Fat 22 g; Chol 79 mg; Sod 894 mg.

LAZY-DAY LASAGNA

4 ounces uncooked
lasagna noodles
1 16-ounce jar spaghetti
sauce
1 pint Basic Ground Beef
Mixture (below)

$^1/_2$ teaspoon oregano
1 cup cream-style
cottage cheese
6 ounces mozzarella
cheese, sliced

Cook noodles using package directions; rinse with cold water and drain. Combine spaghetti sauce, Ground Beef Mixture and oregano in 2-quart glass dish. Microwave, covered with plastic wrap, on Medium-High for 10 minutes, stirring 3 times. Layer noodles, cottage cheese, sauce and mozzarella cheese $^1/_2$ at a time in greased 6x10-inch glass dish. Microwave, covered, on Medium-High for 10 minutes, turning dish once. Let stand for 10 minutes before serving. Yield: 6 servings.

Approx Per Serving: Cal 413; Prot 27 g; Carbo 29 g; Fiber 1 g;
T Fat 21 g; Chol 71 mg; Sod 671 mg.

BASIC GROUND BEEF MIXTURE

2 pounds lean ground
beef
1 cup chopped celery

1 cup chopped onion
$^1/_2$ cup chopped green
bell pepper

Combine ground beef, celery, onion and green pepper in large glass dish. Microwave on High for 9 minutes, stirring 4 times; drain well. Cool. Spoon into freezer containers; seal. Store in freezer. Use Basic Ground Beef Mixture for spaghetti, sloppy Joes, Stroganoff, chili and casseroles. Yield: 3 pints.

Approx Per Pint: Cal 642; Prot 54 g; Carbo 6 g; Fiber 2 g;
T Fat 43 g; Chol 197 mg; Sod 211 mg.

FRIED CHICKEN

1/2 cup dry bread crumbs	1 teaspoon basil
1/2 cup Parmesan cheese	2 teaspoons salt
2 tablespoons oil	1 teaspoon pepper
1/2 teaspoon garlic powder	1 2-pound chicken, cut up

Mix first 6 ingredients in plastic bag. Rinse chicken and pat dry. Add a few pieces at a time to bag, shaking to coat well. Arrange in glass dish with meaty portions toward outside. Cover with waxed paper. Microwave on High for 12 to 14 minutes or until chicken is fork tender. Yield: 5 servings.

Approx Per Serving: Cal 296; Prot 31 g; Carbo 8 g; Fiber <1 g; T Fat 15 g; Chol 88 mg; Sod 1155 mg.

POLYNESIAN CHICKEN

1 pound chicken breast filets	1 medium onion, cut into wedges
1/2 medium green bell pepper	1 8-ounce jar mushroom gravy
1/2 medium red bell pepper	3 tablespoons soy sauce
1/2 cup diagonally sliced celery	1/8 teaspoon ginger
1 cup snow peas	1 8-ounce can juice-pack pineapple chunks, drained

Rinse chicken and pat dry. Slice into 1/2-inch strips; place in 2-quart glass baking dish. Microwave, loosely covered with plastic wrap, on High for 4 minutes or until chicken is no longer pink, stirring twice. Drain chicken and set aside. Cut peppers into chunks. Combine with celery, snow peas and onion in glass dish. Microwave on High for 4 minutes or until tender, stirring once. Add gravy, soy sauce, ginger, pineapple and chicken; mix well. Microwave, covered, for 5 minutes or until heated through. Yield: 4 servings.

Approx Per Serving: Cal 195; Prot 23 g; Carbo 19 g; Fiber 3 g; T Fat 3 g; Chol 49 mg; Sod 1167 mg.

SAUCY HALIBUT

1 pound halibut filets
3 tablespoons
 mayonnaise
2 tablespoons chopped
 onion
1/2 teaspoon dry mustard

1/2 teaspoon dillweed
2 tablespoons melted
 margarine
1 tablespoon freshly
 chopped parsley

Place halibut in 8x8-inch glass baking dish. Mix mayonnaise, onion, dry mustard, dillweed, margarine and parsley in small bowl. Spoon over halibut. Microwave, covered with plastic wrap, on Medium-High for 12 minutes or until fish flakes easily, turning dish once. Yield: 4 servings.

Approx Per Serving: Cal 227; Prot 19 g; Carbo 1 g; Fiber <1 g;
 T Fat 16 g; Chol 35 mg; Sod 175 mg.

SHRIMP DELUXE

1/4 cup dry bread crumbs
1/2 cup butter, softened
1 1/2 tablespoons minced
 parsley
1 tablespoon minced
 onion
2 cloves of garlic, minced
1/4 teaspoon salt

1/4 teaspoon pepper
1/4 teaspoon
 Worcestershire sauce
1 1/2 pounds shrimp,
 peeled
1/4 cup white wine
1/4 cup dry bread crumbs
Paprika to taste

Combine 1/4 cup bread crumbs, butter, parsley, onion, garlic, salt, pepper and Worcestershire sauce in bowl; mix well. Shape into roll 2 inches in diameter on waxed paper. Chill, wrapped, in refrigerator. Place shrimp in 4 glass ramekins. Sprinkle with wine. Slice chilled butter mixture. Place on shrimp. Top with 1/4 cup bread crumbs and paprika. Microwave on High for 5 to 8 minutes or until shrimp are cooked through and butter is bubbly. Yield: 4 servings.

Approx Per Serving: Cal 400; Prot 31 g; Carbo 10 g; Fiber 1 g;
 T Fat 25 g; Chol 328 mg; Sod 728 mg.

HERBED CHEESE OMELET

3 eggs
3 tablespoons milk
1/4 teaspoon basil or
  dillweed
1/4 teaspoon salt

1/8 teaspoon pepper
1 tablespoon butter
1/2 cup shredded Cheddar
  cheese

Beat eggs with milk and seasonings in bowl. Microwave butter on High in glass pie plate for 1 minute. Add egg mixture. Microwave, loosely covered, on Medium-High for 3 minutes, stirring once. Top with cheese. Microwave for 30 seconds or until cheese is melted. Let stand, covered, for 2 minutes. Yield: 2 servings.

Approx Per Serving: Cal 297; Prot 17 g; Carbo 2 g; Fiber 0 g;
    T Fat 24 g; Chol 368 mg; Sod 603 mg.

CALICO BEAN POT

8 slices bacon
1 cup chopped onion
1 16-ounce can cut
  green beans
1 16-ounce can kidney
  beans
1 16-ounce can butter
  beans

1 16-ounce can baby
  lima beans
1 16-ounce can pork
  and beans
1/2 teaspoon garlic salt
1/2 teaspoon dry mustard

Place bacon in 3-quart glass baking dish. Microwave on High for 4 minutes or until crisp; drain, crumble and set aside. Add onion to bacon drippings. Microwave for 3 minutes, stirring once. Drain green beans, kidney beans, butter beans and lima beans. Add drained beans and undrained pork and beans to onion; mix well. Microwave, covered, on Medium for 30 minutes, stirring once. Let stand for 10 minutes. Sprinkle bacon over top. Yield: 12 servings.

Approx Per Serving: Cal 169; Prot 10 g; Carbo 28 g; Fiber 11 g;
    T Fat 3 g; Chol 6 mg; Sod 760 mg.

HOT BROCCOLI VINAIGRETTE

1 bunch broccoli
1 small red onion
3/4 cup Italian salad
  dressing

1/4 cup toasted sesame
  seed

Cut flowerets from broccoli. Slice broccoli stalks and onion; place in shallow glass baking dish. Arrange flowerets around outer edge. Drizzle salad dressing over vegetables. Microwave, loosely covered with plastic wrap, on High for 5 to 7 minutes or until tender-crisp, turning dish every 2 minutes. Let stand for 2 minutes. Sprinkle with sesame seed. Serve hot or at room temperature, as a vegetable or salad. Yield: 4 servings.

Approx Per Serving: Cal 295; Prot 6 g; Carbo 12 g; Fiber 4 g;
  T Fat 32 g; Chol 0 mg; Sod 244 mg.

SPECIAL CAULIFLOWER

1 head cauliflower
1/2 cup mayonnaise
1 teaspoon prepared
  mustard

1/2 to 1 teaspoon dry
  mustard
1 cup shredded American
  cheese

Wash cauliflower. Place whole undrained cauliflower in glass baking dish. Microwave, tightly covered, on High for 7 to 8 minutes. Combine mayonnaise, prepared mustard and dry mustard in bowl; mix well. Spread over cauliflower. Sprinkle with cheese. Microwave on High for 1 minute or just until cheese is melted. Garnish with green and red pepper strips. Yield: 4 servings.

Approx Per Serving: Cal 328; Prot 9 g; Carbo 6 g; Fiber 3 g;
  T Fat 31 g; Chol 43 mg; Sod 592 mg.

GLAZED POTATOES AND CARROTS

1¹/₂ cups coarsely
  chopped peeled
  potatoes
1¹/₂ cups 1-inch carrot
  sticks

2 tablespoons honey
1 tablespoon lemon juice
2 tablespoons butter
¹/₄ teaspoon salt

Arrange potatoes in center and carrots around outer edge of 1¹/₂-quart glass casserole. Add honey, lemon juice and butter. Microwave, covered with plastic wrap, on High for 10 minutes, turning dish once. Let stand for 5 minutes. Season with salt and favorite seasonings to taste. Yield: 4 servings.

Approx Per Serving: Cal 156; Prot 2 g; Carbo 26 g; Fiber 2 g;
    T Fat 6 g; Chol 16 mg; Sod 199 mg.

SWEET POTATO AND PECAN BALLS

1 cup mashed cooked
  sweet potato
¹/₄ teaspoon salt
¹/₄ teaspoon nutmeg
1 egg, beaten
³/₄ cup finely chopped
  pecans

2 tablespoons melted
  butter
¹/₄ cup packed brown
  sugar
1¹/₂ tablespoons light
  corn syrup

Mix sweet potato, salt and nutmeg in bowl. Shape into 2-inch balls. Dip into egg; coat with pecans. Arrange in 7x12-inch glass baking dish. Blend butter, brown sugar and corn syrup in bowl; drizzle over sweet potato balls. Microwave on High for 4 minutes. Let stand for 2 minutes. Yield: 5 servings.

Approx Per Serving: Cal 285; Prot 4 g; Carbo 30 g; Fiber 2 g;
    T Fat 18 g; Chol 55 mg; Sod 205 mg.

SPRING VEGETABLE MEDLEY

2 tablespoons butter
8 ounces fresh
  asparagus spears
1/2 teaspoon basil
Pepper to taste

8 ounces fresh
  mushrooms, sliced
1 tomato, cut into wedges
1/2 teaspoon salt

Microwave butter in 1¹/₂-quart glass casserole on High for 30 seconds. Cut asparagus into 2-inch lengths. Add to casserole with basil and pepper; toss lightly. Microwave, covered with plastic wrap, for 3 minutes. Add mushrooms; toss lightly. Microwave, covered, for 3 minutes. Stir in tomato. Microwave, covered, for 1¹/₂ minutes. Add salt; mix lightly. Let stand, covered, for 3 minutes. Yield: 3 servings.

Approx Per Serving: Cal 112; Prot 4 g; Carbo 8 g; Fiber 3 g;
    T Fat 8 g; Chol 21 mg; Sod 427 mg.

STICKY BUNS

1/3 cup packed brown
  sugar
3 tablespoons margarine

1 tablespoon water
1/3 cup chopped pecans
1 10-count can biscuits

Combine brown sugar, margarine and water in glass baking dish. Microwave on Medium-High for 2 minutes or just until butter is melted. Mix well, spreading evenly. Sprinkle pecans in prepared dish. Arrange biscuits over pecans. Microwave on Medium-High for 4 to 5 minutes or until firm. Let stand for 2 minutes. Invert onto serving plate. Serve immediately. Yield: 10 servings.

Approx Per Serving: Cal 149; Prot 2 g; Carbo 18 g; Fiber 1 g;
    T Fat 8 g; Chol 1 mg; Sod 292 mg.

BLUEBERRY CRUNCH

1/2 cup butter
3/4 cup quick-cooking oats
1 cup packed brown
  sugar
1 cup flour
1 cup sugar
2 tablespoons cornstarch

1 cup water
3 cups fresh or frozen
  blueberries
1/2 teaspoon vanilla
  extract
1/4 teaspoon lemon extract

Combine butter, oats, brown sugar and flour in bowl; mix until crumbly. Press half the crumbs into 9x9-inch glass dish. Mix sugar, cornstarch and water in glass bowl. Microwave on High for 2 to 4 minutes or until thick and clear, stirring several times. Stir in blueberries, vanilla extract and lemon extract. Pour over crumbs in dish. Sprinkle remaining crumbs on top. Microwave on High for 8 to 10 minutes. Let stand for 10 minutes. Serve with ice cream. Yield: 6 servings.

Approx Per Serving: Cal 567; Prot 4 g; Carbo 104 g; Fiber 4 g; T Fat 17 g; Chol 41 mg; Sod 151 mg.

BLUEBERRY-LEMON BREAD PUDDING

1/4 cup butter
4 slices bread, cubed
1/2 cup sugar
2 tablespoons lemon juice
1 cup blueberries

1 cup milk
3 eggs
Cinnamon to taste
1 cup warm water

Microwave butter in glass dish on High for 1 minute or until melted. Add bread, sugar, lemon juice and blueberries; toss lightly to mix. Spoon into glass baking dish. Beat milk and eggs in bowl until smooth. Pour over bread mixture. Sprinkle with cinnamon. Pour warm water over top. Microwave on High for 11 to 13 minutes or just until center is softly set. Serve warm or cool. Yield: 6 servings.

Approx Per Serving: Cal 261; Prot 6 g; Carbo 32 g; Fiber 1 g; T Fat 13 g; Chol 133 mg; Sod 214 mg.

MINTED CHOCOLATE PEARS

1 cup sugar
2 cups water
1¹/₂ teaspoons vanilla
  extract
4 small pears

1 7-ounce package
  chocolate-covered
  mint patties
¹/₄ cup cream

Combine sugar, water and vanilla in glass baking dish. Microwave, covered, on High for 5 minutes or until mixture boils. Peel and core pears; cut into halves. Place in hot mixture. Microwave on High for 2 minutes. Microwave on Medium for 5 minutes or until pears are tender. Cool. Combine mint patties and cream in small glass bowl. Microwave on Medium for 2 minutes or until mints are melted; mix well. Drain pears. Place in serving dishes. Top with chocolate mint sauce. Serve with whipped topping. Yield: 4 servings.

Approx Per Serving: Cal 550; Prot 2 g; Carbo 116 g; Fiber 5 g;
  T Fat 11 g; Chol 20 mg; Sod 99 mg.

CREAMY FUDGE

1 1-pound package
  confectioners' sugar
¹/₃ cup baking cocoa
¹/₄ cup evaporated milk

1 stick butter, sliced
1 teaspoon vanilla extract
¹/₂ cup chopped pecans

Mix confectioners' sugar and cocoa in greased 8x8-inch glass baking dish. Add evaporated milk and butter; do not mix. Microwave on High for 2 minutes or until butter is melted. Stir until mixed. Add vanilla and pecans; mix well. Spread evenly in dish. Chill for 1 hour. Cut into squares. Yield: 24 ounces.

Approx Per Ounce: Cal 145; Prot 1 g; Carbo 24 g; Fiber 1 g;
  T Fat 6 g; Chol 11 mg; Sod 36 mg.

PEANUT TURTLES

2 cups milk chocolate
 chips
2 tablespoons shortening
1 14-ounce package
 caramels

5 tablespoons margarine
2 tablespoons water
1 cup coarsely chopped
 peanuts

Microwave chocolate chips and shortening in glass bowl on Medium for 1 minute or until melted; stir until blended. Spread half the mixture in foil-lined 8x8-inch dish. Chill until firm. Microwave caramels, margarine and water in glass bowl on Medium for 1 1/2 minutes or until caramels melt, stirring occasionally. Mix in peanuts. Spread over chocolate layer. Chill until firm. Microwave remaining chocolate mixture for 30 seconds or until melted. Spread over caramel layer. Chill until firm. Cut into 1-inch squares. Store in refrigerator. Yield: 64 servings.

Approx Per Serving: Cal 77; Prot 1 g; Carbo 8 g; Fiber <1 g;
 T Fat 5 g; Chol <1 mg; Sod 25 mg.

LEMON BARS

1/3 cup butter
1 1/2 cups shortbread
 cookie crumbs
1 teaspoon grated lemon
 rind

1 14-ounce can
 sweetened condensed
 milk
1/2 cup lemon juice

Microwave butter on High in 8x8-inch glass baking dish for 45 seconds or until melted. Stir in crumbs and lemon rind. Reserve 1/4 cup mixture. Press remaining mixture evenly into dish. Beat condensed milk and lemon juice in bowl until smooth. Pour over crumb mixture. Sprinkle reserved crumb mixture over top. Microwave on Medium-High for 10 minutes, turning dish once. Cool. Cut into squares. Store in refrigerator. Yield: 16 servings.

Approx Per Serving: Cal 195; Prot 3 g; Carbo 25 g; Fiber <1 g;
 T Fat 10 g; Chol 33 mg; Sod 127 mg.

Energy-Saving Outdoor Cooking

HOT KNAPSACK SALAD

2 bananas
2 plums
2 peaches
1 8-ounce can
   pineapple, drained

1/4 cup packed brown
   sugar
1/4 cup margarine
4 teaspoons lemon juice

Cut fresh fruit into chunks; divide among 4 pieces of heavy-duty foil. Add pineapple, brown sugar, margarine and lemon juice. Fold foil, sealing tightly. Attach packets to sticks or place packets on grill. Cook over medium coals for 10 minutes or until heated through. Yield: 4 servings.

Approx Per Serving: Cal 273; Prot 2 g; Carbo 44 g; Fiber 3 g;
    T Fat 12 g; Chol 0 mg; Sod 141 mg.

BEEF ALAMO

1 pound beef flank steak
1/2 cup hot mustard
12 flour tortillas
1 red onion, chopped

2 medium tomatoes,
   chopped
1 4-ounce can chopped
   green chilies

Score steak diagonally on both sides at 1-inch intervals in diamond pattern. Spread mustard over both sides. Chill, covered, for several hours. Grill over medium-hot coals for 8 to 10 minutes on each side. Stack tortillas; wrap in foil. Place on edge of grill to warm. Cut steak into thin slices. Spoon onto warm tortillas. Top with mixture of onion, tomatoes and chilies. Roll tortillas to enclose filling. Yield: 6 servings.

Approx Per Serving: Cal 473; Prot 24 g; Carbo 68 g; Fiber 5 g;
    T Fat 14 g; Chol 43 mg; Sod 720 mg.

STEAK STRIPS EN BROCHETTE

2 pounds round steak
1 cup Russian salad
   dressing
2 tablespoons lemon juice

12 medium fresh
   mushrooms
12 cherry tomatoes

Cut steak into ¼-inch strips; place in plastic bag. Add salad dressing and lemon juice; mix well. Press out air; seal bag securely. Marinate in refrigerator for 4 hours to overnight. Drain, reserving marinade. Thread beef strips alternately with mushrooms and tomatoes onto six 15-inch skewers. Place on grill. Grill over medium coals for 3 minutes, brushing with marinade occasionally. Turn skewers and brush with marinade. Grill for 3 to 4 minutes or until done to taste, brushing occasionally with marinade. Yield: 6 servings.

Approx Per Serving: Cal 426; Prot 30 g; Carbo 10 g; Fiber 2 g;
   T Fat 30 g; Chol 112 mg; Sod 409 mg.
   Nutritional information includes entire amount of marinade.

CAMPFIRE STEW

1 3-pound chuck roast
1 cup flour
Salt and pepper to taste
½ cup oil
6 potatoes, chopped

6 carrots, sliced
2 onions, sliced
2 stalks celery, sliced
1 bay leaf
3 cups water

Trim roast and cut into bite-sized pieces. Coat with mixture of flour, salt and pepper. Brown in hot oil in Dutch oven over hot coals, stirring frequently. Add potatoes, carrots, onions, celery, bay leaf and water; mix well. Cook, covered, over hot coals for 4 hours or until tender, stirring occasionally and adding water if necessary. Remove bay leaf.
Yield: 15 servings.

Approx Per Serving: Cal 322; Prot 20 g; Carbo 31 g; Fiber 3 g;
   T Fat 13 g; Chol 51 mg; Sod 49 mg.

GREEN PEPPER BURGERS

1 pound ground beef
1 medium onion, minced
1/2 green bell pepper,
  minced

2 cloves of garlic, minced
2 teaspoons cumin
2 teaspoons coriander
Salt and pepper to taste

Combine ground beef, onion, green pepper, garlic and seasonings in bowl; mix well. Shape into patties. Grill over hot coals until done to taste. Serve on sandwich buns, in flour tortillas or in pita pockets. Yield: 6 servings.

Approx Per Serving: Cal 166; Prot 15 g; Carbo 3 g; Fiber 1 g;
    T Fat 11 g; Chol 49 mg; Sod 44 mg.

PIZZA LOAVES

1 pound ground beef
1/2 cup chopped onion
1 8-ounce can pizza
  sauce
1/2 teaspoon each
  oregano and salt

1/4 cup sliced stuffed
  olives
1 loaf French bread, split
  lengthwise
1 cup shredded Muenster
  cheese

Brown ground beef and onion in skillet, stirring frequently. Stir in pizza sauce, oregano, salt and olives. Place each bread half on square of foil. Spoon ground beef mixture over bread. Sprinkle with cheese; seal foil tightly. Place on grill over low coals. Cook for 15 minutes or until heated through. Yield: 6 servings.

Approx Per Serving: Cal 495; Prot 26 g; Carbo 46 g; Fiber 3 g;
    T Fat 23 g; Chol 67 mg; Sod 1193 mg.

 Use reusable dishes, napkins and utensils instead of paper products at picnics or cookouts.

HAM DINNER

16 cabbage leaves
1 16-ounce can cut
   green beans, drained

1 16-ounce can whole
   kernel corn, drained
4 cups chopped ham

Cut heavy-duty foil into eight 18-inch pieces. Place 1 cabbage leaf on each piece of foil. Layer green beans, corn and ham in cabbage leaves; top with remaining cabbage leaves. Seal foil tightly. Place in hot coals. Cook for 5 to 10 minutes on each side or until heated through. Cabbage keeps ham and vegetables from burning. May substitute hot dogs or ground beef patties for ham and favorite vegetables for beans and corn. Yield: 8 servings.

Approx Per Serving: Cal 170; Prot 20 g; Carbo 14 g; Fiber 2 g;
   T Fat 5 g; Chol 39 mg; Sod 1206 mg.

TERIYAKI PORK CHOPS

$1/2$ cup teriyaki sauce
$1/4$ cup minced green
   onions
$1/4$ cup lemon juice
2 tablespoons peanut oil

4 cloves of garlic, minced
2 teaspoons crushed red
   pepper
4 $3/4$-inch pork chops

Combine teriyaki sauce, green onions, lemon juice, peanut oil, garlic and red pepper in small bowl; mix well. Pour over pork chops in shallow dish. Marinate in refrigerator overnight, turning occasionally. Drain, reserving marinade. Place pork chops on grill 6 to 8 inches above hot coals. Grill for 30 to 45 minutes or until done to taste, turning and basting frequently with reserved marinade.
Yield: 4 servings.

Approx Per Serving: Cal 328; Prot 34 g; Carbo 8 g; Fiber <1 g;
   T Fat 17 g; Chol 98 mg; Sod 1458 mg.
   Nutritional information includes entire amount of marinade.

CHILI DOGS IN BLANKETS

10 6-inch flour tortillas
10 hot dogs
1 15-ounce can chili
  with beans

1½ cups shredded
  American cheese

Place each tortilla on sheet of heavy-duty foil. Place hot dog in center of each tortilla. Top each with 2 tablespoons chili and 2 tablespoons cheese. Roll to enclose filling; secure with wooden picks. Wrap foil tightly. Place on grill 4 to 6 inches from hot coals. Grill for 10 to 15 minutes or until heated through. Serve with sour cream. Yield: 10 servings.

Approx Per Serving: Cal 315; Prot 13 g; Carbo 17 g; Fiber 2 g;
  T Fat 22 g; Chol 46 mg; Sod 1044 mg.

FOILED CHICKEN

4 chicken thighs
4 chicken legs
1 onion, chopped
2 carrots, sliced
8 mushrooms, sliced

1 16-ounce can green
  beans, drained
1 10-ounce can cream
  of celery soup

Cut heavy-duty foil into four 12x16-inch pieces. Rinse chicken and pat dry. Place 1 thigh and 1 leg on each piece of foil. Combine onion, carrots, mushrooms, green beans and soup in bowl; mix well. Spoon evenly over chicken; seal foil tightly. Grill over hot coals for 2 hours or until chicken is tender. Yield: 4 servings.

Approx Per Serving: Cal 506; Prot 43 g; Carbo 18 g; Fiber 4 g;
  T Fat 29 g; Chol 150 mg; Sod 958 mg.

BARBECUED SHERRIED CHICKEN

8 chicken quarters
Salt and pepper to taste
1 cup margarine
1/2 cup lemon juice

1 tablespoon
  Worcestershire sauce
Tabasco sauce to taste
1/4 cup cooking Sherry

Rinse chicken and pat dry. Season with salt and pepper. Combine margarine, lemon juice, Worcestershire sauce, Tabasco sauce and wine in saucepan. Cook over low heat until margarine melts; mix well. Brush over chicken. Place chicken on grill. Add 3 presoaked hickory chips to coals. Grill over low coals for 1 1/2 hours or until chicken is tender, turning and basting frequently. Yield: 8 servings.

Approx Per Serving: Cal 379; Prot 25 g; Carbo 2 g; Fiber <1 g;
  T Fat 29 g; Chol 76 mg; Sod 360 mg.
  Nutritional information includes entire amount of
  barbecue sauce.

GRILLED LEMON CHICKEN

1 cup orange juice
1/3 cup lemon juice
1/4 cup oil

2 tablespoons soy sauce
1 teaspoon lemon pepper
6 chicken breast filets

Combine orange juice, lemon juice, oil, soy sauce and lemon pepper in bowl; mix well. Rinse chicken and pat dry. Add to marinade, turning to coat well. Marinate in refrigerator for 2 hours to overnight. Grill chicken over hot coals for 20 minutes or until tender, brushing occasionally with marinade. Yield: 6 servings.

Approx Per Serving: Cal 197; Prot 20 g; Carbo 6 g; Fiber <1 g;
  T Fat 10 g; Chol 49 mg; Sod 399 mg.
  Nutritional information includes entire amount of marinade.

BACKYARD SHRIMP

3 pounds fresh shrimp,
  peeled
2/3 cup melted margarine
1/4 cup chopped onion
1/4 cup chili sauce
1/2 teaspoon garlic powder

Tabasco sauce and
  Worcestershire sauce
  to taste
1/3 cup chopped parsley
2 tablespoons lemon juice

Cut heavy-duty foil into six 12x12-inch squares. Place shrimp on foil. Combine margarine, onion, chili sauce, garlic powder, Tabasco sauce, Worcestershire sauce, parsley and lemon juice in bowl; mix well. Spoon over shrimp; seal with double folds. Place on grill 4 inches from hot coals. Grill for 20 minutes or until done to taste. Yield: 8 servings.

Approx Per Serving: Cal 291; Prot 28 g; Carbo 4 g; Fiber <1 g;
  T Fat 17 g; Chol 207 mg; Sod 493 mg.
  Nutritional information includes entire amount of
  cooking sauce.

SALMON AND ZUCCHINI BUNDLES

4 6-ounce salmon steaks
1 10-ounce can tomato
  soup
1/4 teaspoon garlic powder

1 medium zucchini, thinly
  sliced
1/4 cup Parmesan cheese

Cut heavy-duty foil into four 14x14-inch squares. Place 1 salmon steak on each square. Combine soup, garlic powder, zucchini and cheese in bowl; mix well. Spoon over salmon; seal with double fold. Place on grill 4 inches from hot coals. Grill for 25 minutes. Yield: 4 servings.

Approx Per Serving: Cal 269; Prot 31 g; Carbo 11 g; Fiber 1 g;
  T Fat 11 g; Chol 79 mg; Sod 647 mg.

GRILLED LEMON SNAPPER

¹/₂ cup lemon juice
Salt and pepper to taste
¹/₂ teaspoon thyme
1¹/₂ pounds red snapper
**   filets**

2 tablespoons melted
**   margarine**

Combine lemon juice, salt, pepper and thyme in dish; mix well. Add fish, turning to coat well. Marinate, covered, in refrigerator for 1 hour, turning 3 times; drain. Brush fish with melted margarine. Place on grill over hot coals. Grill for 5 minutes on each side or until fish flakes easily, turning once. Yield: 4 servings.

Approx Per Serving: Cal 195; Prot 28 g; Carbo 3 g; Fiber <1 g;
    T Fat 8 g; Chol 50 mg; Sod 154 mg.

CORN IN HUSKS

6 ears unhusked corn
¹/₄ cup margarine,
**   softened**

Salt and pepper to taste

Pull corn husks back; discard silks. Pull husks back over corn; tie with string. Soak in ice water to cover for 30 minutes to 2 hours; drain. Place on grill over hot coals. Grill for 10 to 15 minutes or until husks are browned, turning several times. Remove husks. Serve with margarine, salt and pepper. Yield: 6 servings.

Approx Per Serving: Cal 151; Prot 3 g; Carbo 20 g; Fiber 3 g;
    T Fat 9 g; Chol 0 mg; Sod 102 mg.

GRILLED ONIONS

4 large Vidalia onions
4 teaspoons butter

4 beef bouillon cubes
Salt and pepper to taste

Skin and rinse onions; remove cores. Place each on double thickness of heavy-duty foil. Place butter and bouillon cubes in centers of onions; seal foil securely. Grill over hot coals for 45 minutes. Yield: 4 servings.

Approx Per Serving: Cal 94; Prot 3 g; Carbo 12 g; Fiber 3 g;
    T Fat 4 g; Chol 10 mg; Sod 899 mg.

CREAMY POTATO BAKE

5 medium potatoes
1 medium onion, sliced
6 tablespoons margarine
Salt and pepper to taste
1/3 cup shredded Cheddar
  cheese

2 tablespoons chopped
  parsley
1 tablespoon
  Worcestershire sauce
1/3 cup chicken broth

Peel and slice potatoes. Place potatoes and onion on 18x22-inch piece of heavy-duty foil. Dot with margarine. Sprinkle with salt, pepper, cheese, parsley and Worcestershire sauce. Fold edges up; add broth carefully. Seal foil tightly. Grill over medium-hot coals in covered grill for 35 minutes or until potatoes are tender. Yield: 6 servings.

Approx Per Serving: Cal 324; Prot 6 g; Carbo 45 g; Fiber 4 g;
    T Fat 14 g; Chol 7 mg; Sod 254 mg.

ZUCCHINI PARMESAN

1/2 **cup Parmesan cheese**	1/2 **cup chopped onion**
1 medium zucchini, sliced	**Salt and pepper to taste**

Spray large piece of foil with nonstick cooking spray. Sprinkle 1/4 cup cheese onto foil. Add zucchini and onion. Sprinkle with remaining cheese, salt and pepper; seal foil. Place on grill over hot coals. Grill for 20 to 30 minutes or until tender, turning packet once or twice. Yield: 4 servings.

Approx Per Serving: Cal 62; Prot 5 g; Carbo 4 g; Fiber 1 g;
    T Fat 3 g; Chol 8 mg; Sod 190 mg.

CHEESY BREAD KABOBS

1 5-ounce jar sharp American cheese spread	**1 tablespoon sliced green onions**
1 tablespoon margarine, softened	1/4 **teaspoon tarragon**
Garlic powder to taste	1/2 **teaspoon parsley flakes**
	8 slices French bread

Combine cheese spread, margarine, garlic powder, green onions, tarragon and parsley flakes in bowl; mix well. Spread on 1 side of bread slices. Stack 4 slices together; spread remaining cheese mixture on tops and bottoms of stacks. Cut each stack into quarters. Thread onto skewers. Grill over medium coals for 6 to 7 minutes or until lightly toasted, turning frequently. Yield: 8 servings.

Approx Per Serving: Cal 171; Prot 7 g; Carbo 19 g; Fiber 1 g;
    T Fat 7 g; Chol 11 mg; Sod 430 mg.

GRILLED FRENCH BREAD

1 long loaf French bread
1/2 cup margarine,
  softened

1 clove of garlic, crushed
1/3 cup Parmesan cheese

    Slice loaf into halves lengthwise. Mix margarine and garlic in small bowl. Spread over cut sides of bread; sprinkle with cheese. Place cut sides together. Wrap in heavy-duty foil. Place on grill 5 inches from medium coals. Heat for 15 minutes, turning occasionally. May add other seasonings as desired. Yield: 6 servings.

Approx Per Serving: Cal 373; Prot 9 g; Carbo 39 g; Fiber 2 g;
    T Fat 19 g; Chol 3 mg; Sod 700 mg.

BANANA BOATS

4 bananas
40 miniature
  marshmallows

4 milk chocolate bars,
  broken

    Peel back 1 section banana peel from each banana; do not remove. Cut lengthwise wedge-shaped section from each banana. Place marshmallows and chocolate in cavities in bananas. Replace peel section; wrap each banana tightly in heavy-duty foil. Place on grill over coals or in low coals. Bake for 3 minutes or until chocolate and marshmallows melt. Yield: 4 servings.

Approx Per Serving: Cal 367; Prot 4 g; Carbo 62 g; Fiber 3 g;
    T Fat 14 g; Chol 9 mg; Sod 48 mg.

DUTCH OVEN COBBLER

1 21-ounce can cherry
   pie filling
¹/₄ cup sugar
1 12-ounce package
   baking mix

¹/₄ cup melted margarine
2 tablespoons
   cinnamon-sugar

Preheat 20 charcoal briquettes. Line Dutch oven with foil. Preheat Dutch oven near coals. Combine pie filling and sugar in Dutch oven. Heat over 8 coals until mixture bubbles. Combine baking mix with enough water to make soft dough in bowl; mix well. Drop by spoonfuls over cherry mixture. Cover with top of oven. Place remaining coals on top of oven. Bake for 15 to 20 minutes or until golden brown. Brush with margarine; sprinkle with cinnamon-sugar. Yield: 8 servings.

Approx Per Serving: Cal 362; Prot 4 g; Carbo 60 g; Fiber 1 g;
    T Fat 13 g; Chol 0 mg; Sod 685 mg.

CAMPFIRE CUPCAKES

1 2-layer package lemon
   cake mix

15 oranges

Prepare cake mix using package directions. Cut oranges into halves. Scoop out pulp and reserve for another purpose; reserve orange shells. Fill each orange shell ²/₃ full with cake batter. Wrap each loosely in foil. Place over medium coals. Bake for 20 minutes or until cupcakes test done. Yield: 30 servings.

Approx Per Serving: Cal 154; Prot 2 g; Carbo 29 g; Fiber 2 g;
    T Fat 4 g; Chol 0 mg; Sod 84 mg.

Easy Equivalent Chart

	When the recipe calls for	Use
Baking	¹/₂ cup butter	4 ounces
	2 cups butter	1 pound
	4 cups all-purpose flour	1 pound
	4¹/₂ to 5 cups sifted cake flour	1 pound
	1 square chocolate	1 ounce
	1 cup semisweet chocolate chips	6 ounces
	4 cups marshmallows	1 pound
	2¹/₄ cups packed brown sugar	1 pound
	4 cups confectioners' sugar	1 pound
	2 cups granulated sugar	1 pound
Cereal – Bread	1 cup fine dry bread crumbs	4 to 5 slices
	1 cup soft bread crumbs	2 slices
	1 cup small bread cubes	2 slices
	1 cup fine cracker crumbs	28 saltines
	1 cup fine graham cracker crumbs	15 crackers
	1 cup vanilla wafer crumbs	22 wafers
	1 cup crushed cornflakes	3 cups uncrushed
	4 cups cooked macaroni	8 ounces uncooked
	3¹/₂ cups cooked rice	1 cup uncooked
Dairy	1 cup shredded cheese	4 ounces
	1 cup cottage cheese	8 ounces
	1 cup sour cream	8 ounces
	1 cup whipped cream	¹/₂ cup heavy cream
	²/₃ cup evaporated milk	1 small can
	1²/₃ cups evaporated milk	1 13-ounce can
Fruit	4 cups sliced or chopped apples	4 medium
	1 cup mashed bananas	3 medium
	2 cups pitted cherries	4 cups unpitted
	2¹/₂ cups shredded coconut	8 ounces
	4 cups cranberries	1 pound
	1 cup pitted dates	1 8-ounce package
	3 to 4 tablespoons lemon juice plus 1 tablespoon grated lemon rind	1 lemon
	¹/₃ cup orange juice plus 2 teaspoons grated orange rind	1 orange
	4 cups sliced peaches	8 medium
	2 cups pitted prunes	1 12-ounce package
	3 cups raisins	1 15-ounce package

	When the recipe calls for	Use
Meats	4 cups chopped cooked chicken 3 cups chopped cooked meat 2 cups cooked ground meat	1 5-pound chicken 1 pound, cooked 1 pound, cooked
Nuts	1 cup chopped nuts	4 ounces shelled 1 pound unshelled
Vegetables	2 cups cooked green beans 2¹/₂ cups lima beans or red beans 4 cups shredded cabbage 1 cup grated carrot 8 ounces fresh mushrooms 1 cup chopped onion 4 cups sliced or chopped potatoes 2 cups canned tomatoes	¹/₂ pound fresh or 1 16-ounce can 1 cup dried, cooked 1 pound 1 large 1 4-ounce can 1 large 4 medium 1 16-ounce can

Measurement Equivalents

1 tablespoon = 3 teaspoons
2 tablespoons = 1 ounce
4 tablespoons = ¹/₄ cup
5¹/₃ tablespoons = ¹/₃ cup
8 tablespoons = ¹/₂ cup
12 tablespoons = ³/₄ cup
16 tablespoons = 1 cup
1 cup = 8 ounces or ¹/₂ pint
4 cups = 1 quart
4 quarts = 1 gallon

1 6¹/₂ to 8-ounce can = 1 cup
1 10¹/₂ to 12-ounce can = 1¹/₄ cups
1 14 to 16-ounce can = 1³/₄ cups
1 16 to 17-ounce can = 2 cups
1 18 to 20-ounce can = 2¹/₂ cups
1 29-ounce can = 3¹/₂ cups
1 46 to 51-ounce can = 5³/₄ cups
1 6¹/₂ to 7¹/₂-pound can or
Number 10 = 12 to 13 cups

Metric Equivalents

Liquid	Dry
1 teaspoon = 5 milliliters 1 tablespoon = 15 milliliters 1 fluid ounce = 30 milliliters 1 cup = 250 milliliters 1 pint = 500 milliliters	1 quart = 1 liter 1 ounce = 30 grams 1 pound = 450 grams 2.2 pounds = 1 kilogram

NOTE: The metric measures are approximate benchmarks for purposes of
home food preparation.

Fast Substitution Chart

	Instead of	Use
Baking	1 teaspoon baking powder	1/4 teaspoon soda plus 1/2 teaspoon cream of tartar
	1 tablespoon cornstarch (for thickening)	2 tablespoons flour or 1 tablespoon tapioca
	1 cup sifted all-purpose flour	1 cup plus 2 tablespoons sifted cake flour
	1 cup sifted cake flour	1 cup minus 2 tablespoons sifted all-purpose flour
	1 cup dry bread crumbs	3/4 cup cracker crumbs
Dairy	1 cup buttermilk	1 cup sour milk or 1 cup yogurt
	1 cup heavy cream	3/4 cup skim milk plus 1/3 cup butter
	1 cup light cream	7/8 cup skim milk plus 3 tablespoons butter
	1 cup sour cream	7/8 cup sour milk plus 3 tablespoons butter
	1 cup sour milk	1 cup milk plus 1 tablespoon vinegar or lemon juice or 1 cup buttermilk
Seasoning	1 teaspoon allspice	1/2 teaspoon cinnamon plus 1/8 teaspoon cloves
	1 cup catsup	1 cup tomato sauce plus 1/2 cup sugar plus 2 tablespoons vinegar
	1 clove of garlic	1/8 teaspoon garlic powder or 1/8 teaspoon instant minced garlic or 3/4 teaspoon garlic salt
	1 teaspoon Italian spice	1/4 teaspoon each oregano, basil, thyme, rosemary plus dash of cayenne
	1 teaspoon lemon juice	1/2 teaspoon vinegar
	1 tablespoon mustard	1 teaspoon dry mustard
	1 medium onion	1 tablespoon dried minced onion or 1 teaspoon onion powder
Sweet	1 1-ounce square chocolate	1/4 cup cocoa plus 1 teaspoon shortening
	1 2/3 ounces semisweet chocolate	1 ounce unsweetened chocolate plus 4 teaspoons granulated sugar
	1 cup honey	1 to 1 1/4 cups sugar plus 1/4 cup liquid or 1 cup corn syrup or molasses
	1 cup granulated sugar	1 cup packed brown sugar or 1 cup honey minus 1/4 cup liquid

Index

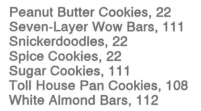

FAVORITE RECIPES® PRESS COOKBOOKS

For Your Collection
or
As A Gift

For a List of Available Books with
Ordering Information

Write to:
Favorite Recipes® Press
P.O. Box 305142
Nashville, TN 37230

or

Call Toll-free
1-800-251-1542